BOURNEMOUTH & SOUTHAMPTON STEAM
1947-1967

'Battle of Britain' 4-6-2 No 34059 *Sir Archibald Sinclair* gallops along Coy Pond embankment near journey's end with the down 'Bournemouth Belle' on 26 August 1956.

BOURNEMOUTH &
SOUTHAMPTON STEAM
1947-1967

Colin Boocock

LONDON

IAN ALLAN LTD

Contents

Cover, above:
The superb upper-quadrant signal gantry at Southampton Central has at last gone. Under it in 1956 departs No 34039 *Boscastle* **with the Brighton-Plymouth through train,** *Lord Nelson* **is signalled away with the 11.30am Waterloo-Bournemouth while** *Sir Francis Drake* **waits in the bay.**

Cover, below:
The atmosphere of steam is intense at the east end of Bournemouth Central in August 1956 as No 35018 *British India Line* **prepares to restart the up Belle. No 30783** *Sir Gillemere* **waits on the up through line with a fitted freight.**

Previous page:
No 30862 *Lord Collingwood* **accelerates the 5pm from Bournemouth West to Waterloo past Bevois Park yard and the upper reaches of Southampton Water as it approaches St Denys on 19 September 1959.**

Preface	5
Railway Port — Railway Resort	8
Pullman Perfection	15
Steam Centre: Bournemouth	23
Steam Centre: Southampton	32
Steam Centre: Eastleigh	41
Wessex Artery	48
Dorsetway	55
Over the Mendips	64
Branches	71
Cross-Country	79
They also served	85
Appendices	93

All photographs in this book are by the author unless they are otherwise credited.

First published 1985

ISBN 0 7110 1461 2

Published by Ian Allan Ltd, Shepperton, Surrey; and printed by Ian Allan Printing Ltd at their works at Coombelands in Runnymede, England.

Dedication
This book is dedicated to all the members, past and present, of the Bournemouth Railway Club, in grateful recognition of their enthusiasm and fellowship.

Acknowledgements
The author has received willing help with information and photographs from his friends in the Bournemouth Railway Club and from others, and hopes he has omitted no-one from this list:

Mark Abbott, Allan Baker, Nick Bartlett, Ian Foot, Roy Panting, Tony Sterndale, Robin Stieber, Mike Smith, Alan Thorpe, Alan Trickett, and Alan Wild.

The chapter heading 'Pullman Perfection' was first used by O. J. Morris for the title of an early Ian Allan booklet. It is re-used here in his fond memory.

Preface

As a small boy towards the end of the last war I used to visit Weybridge with my father to watch the trains rattle through the cutting. To me, living at Addlestone on a branch line served only by suburban electric trains, the sight of 'Merchant Navy' Pacifics, 'Lord Nelsons' and 'King Arthurs' hammering past Weybridge with Bournemouth trains was an introduction to a thrilling new world.

In 1945 we had our first holiday in Bournemouth. I remember arriving in the West terminus there to see that black 'Merchant Navy' No 21C13 *Blue Funnel Line* had hauled us from London. Our hotel backed on to the railway cutting near the crossroads known to bus conductors as Cemetery Junction. I spent many happy hours at the back fence watching that all-steam railway. When I said to my parents, 'I wish we lived here', little did I know that my father was actively in pursuit of a post in Bournemouth, to where we happily moved before the end of that year!

My first school there was St Clements in Boscombe. Sometimes after school I would visit the home of a friend whose house overlooked the railway. We would stand at the back fence waiting for the 'Bournemouth Belle' to pass. To this day I have a vivid mental picture of an immaculate, malachite green, air-smoothed 'Merchant Navy' surging ahead strongly in front of those gorgeous, slat-sided, chocolate-and-cream, 12-wheeled Pullmans. No other train has ever stirred my emotions more than that superb formation, at least not until the appearance of British Rail's sleek Inter-City 125s or France's TGV.

So if the 'Bournemouth Belle' features unduly prominently in these pages, dear reader please forgive me!

In 1947 I joined the Bournemouth Junior Railway Club, run by the very strict Reverend A. Cunningham-Burley who hired the George Temperance Hall once a month to provide us boys with railway lectures and lantern slides. Here I first met O. J. Morris, whose pictures of prewar Southern Railway trains, I must admit, made me glad to be living in the Bulleid era. However, his photographs in his booklet *My Best Railway Photographs* published by Ian Allan, and in particular the companion volume by the then Canon Eric Treacy, inspired me to try railway photography.

Below:
'Merchant Navy' No 35018 *British India Line* **retains malachite green livery in this 1948 photograph at Bournemouth Central.**

One summer afternoon in 1947 I took my father with his old Nagel folding camera down to Bournemouth Central station. There I photographed two 'King Arthurs' and the 'M7' station shunter, No 112. Now, 10,000 photographs and 38 years later, I still take a camera with me on my travels.

In the early 1950s my travels took me frequently to Dorchester and Weymouth to visit my great aunt, to Salisbury to train watch and to Eastleigh to visit the works and shed. The locomotive works was an enormously awe inspring place to a youngster. This was where one's favourite locomotives came to be stripped down, overhauled and given coats of shining paint.

Many holidays were spent visiting my grandparents in Colne in Lancashire. The journey north to Manchester required us to travel on the 'Pines Express' from Bournemouth West, traversing the whole length of the main line of that beautiful railway, the Somerset & Dorset. My first memory of the 'Pines' I must confess is of drab, dirty maroon corridor coaches hauled by a grimy LMS Class 5, No 5056, but the passage through the Mendip hills placed the S&D firmly in the big

Above:

Supremely Southern, 'King Arthur' 4-6-0 No 789 *Sir Guy* **stands at the Bournemouth Central on a Waterloo-bound semi-fast in the summer of 1947.** *Sidney Boocock*

Above right:

'M7' No 112 was for many years the station shunting engine for Bournemouth Central. This 1947 view shows clearly the view of the locomotive shed that could be had from the down platform extension.

league of railway climbs. Piloting over the top was by Class 2P 4-4-0s until the advent of the smaller BR standard classes. The scenery was magnificent. No wonder so many books have been published on it, though here one chapter must suffice.

By 1954 I had made my career choice in the teeth of the traditions of Bournemouth (Grammar) School. At 16 I became an engineering apprentice at Eastleigh locomotive works. The experience was at once satisfying as it was traumatic. With my middle class background I had to learn to recognise and not hurt a good working man's pride, and to accept that while class differences can and need to be bridged, each man is entitled to uphold the traditions of his upbringing. The lessons of those years have helped me through a very fulfilling railway career that has taken me up through the management ranges via all Regions.

My times at Eastleigh and my college days at Southampton gave me opportunities to photograph the railway scene in those parts, which form more chapters in this album.

My career later brought me back to Eastleigh in time to witness the end of steam in the area. I was able to play a part in the rationalisation of Eastleigh works for its role in the electric age.

It has also been my pleasure to continue my membership of the Bournemouth Railway Club and so keep up to date with the railways of Bournemouth and Southampton through all these years. It is good to have witnessed the benefits of electrification from 1967, the expansion of the Waterloo fasts (91s) in the early 1970s, and BR's fight to obtain new freight business for the modern railway. These developments fully compensate for any regrets I may have had for the passing of the steam age.

Above:
'LMS engines were black and usually dirty'. Class 5 4-6-0 No 4827 stands at the head of the northbound 'Pines Express' at Bournemouth West in 1947.

Railway Port — Railway Resort

The two south coast towns of Bournemouth and Southampton could hardly be more different in character. The great port of Southampton was an obvious target for the 19th century railway builders from London. Bournemouth in those years was a small seaside village clustered around the mouth of a stream.

Today, Southampton has developed as a commercial and industrial centre with its dependence on railways modified. Bournemouth has grown to be a large, somewhat up-market, seaside resort while forming with Poole part of a semi-industrial conurbation.

Bournemouth's early growth was spurred on by the arrival of the railway. Initially however it was ignored. The Southampton & Dorchester Railway had other objectives in view and so succeeded in by-passing the town completely.

Below:
This 1927 aerial photograph of Southampton (Old) Docks shows how prominently the railway featured among the warehouses and wharves. Seven ocean-going liners can be seen. In the centre background is Terminus station and top right the gas holders at Northam. *Hampshire County Libraries*

This marketing mistake (it can only be seen as such in retrospect) was later put right and by 1888 Bournemouth had a direct line to Southampton and London. Such is the inertia of human affairs that the Old Road, as the original Dorchester line via Ringwood was known, led a country by-way type of existence right through the years until the review of routes by Dr Beeching ended it, together with other routes to Salisbury, Swanage, Templecombe and Bath.

Above:
Bournemouth Central in 1905, with 'T9' 4-4-0 No 715 on an up train. Left foreground shows the short down bay siding, long since gone, and in the background the down platform lacks its western extension, added in Southern Railway times.
Dorset County Libraries

Southampton's railway links were spread in many directions. Lines went along both sides of Southampton Water, the east side to Fareham and Portsmouth, the west side from

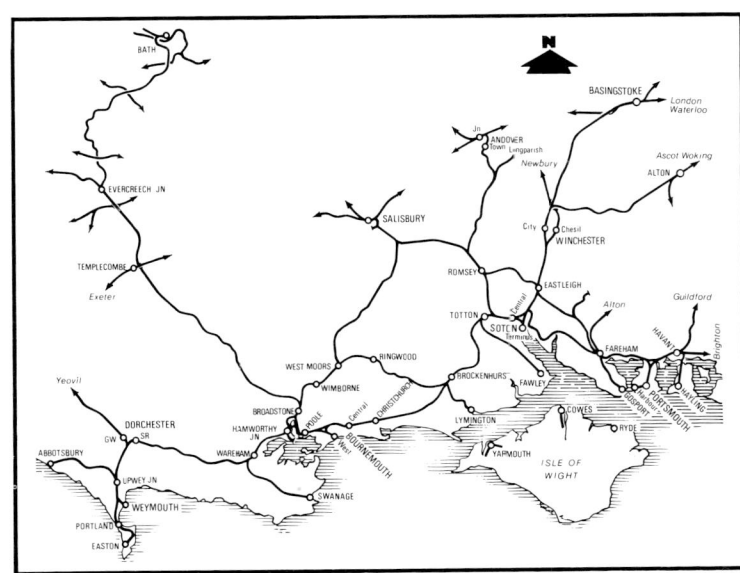

Railways in 1947.

Totton to the villages of Marchwood and Fawley. A route leaving the Bournemouth line at Redbridge headed north to Salisbury, on the Waterloo-Exeter line, where the Great Western met it head on with a line from Bath, permitting through trains from Bristol to Portsmouth. Eastleigh (formerly Bishopstoke), seven miles up the line from Southampton, also had links joining the Salisbury and Portsmouth routes at Romsey and Fareham respectively. The Great Western had a route heading towards Southampton, taken over from the Didcot, Newbury & Southampton Railway which had given up near Winchester and joined its line to the LSW main line at Shawford.

Apart from the DN&S incursion, the GWR never successfully got closer than Dorchester and Salisbury to the area covered by this book. This was all basically London & South Western Railway territory, Southern Railway from 1923. Even the Somerset & Dorset Joint Railway was part Southern, though it did bring locomotives into the area from the London, Midland & Scottish Railway.

If there was a heyday of steam in this area, I believe it was the 1950s. We had Bulleid Pacifics of all types dominating the main line, and most of the former engines back through Maunsell, Urie, Drummond and Adams survived, with the noble exception of the Adams 4-4-0s. Life was fascinating in its variety. Carriages were good as well. From the plushness of the Maunsell stock we progressed to the bright interiors of Bulleid's magnificent Bournemouth six-car restaurant sets introduced in 1946, against which the later BR Mk 1 stock of 1951 were a dull comparison.

The variety was added to by the LMS engines which reached Bournemouth West from the Somerset & Dorset line. I remember being disappointed that LMS engines were black, and usually dirty. They remained foreign and unfamiliar, and were usually kept away from the busy Bournemouth Central station and locomotive yard, being serviced instead at the small shed in the relatively inaccessible Branksome triangle.

LMS wasn't the only set of strange initials to appear on engine tenders in Bournemouth. I remember one Sunday afternoon standing on the Central station's down platform extension that so conveniently flanked the town's large motive power depot when a foreign tender emerged from under Beechy Road bridge. Under the layers of soot and brake block dust could just be discerned the letters GWR, as the first 'Hall' 4-6-0 I had ever seen in Bournemouth came to the depot after terminating its excursion train at Bournemouth West. Through workings from the Western Region came soon, thereafter to be a daily affair when the Newcastle to Bournemouth

Below:
The Didcot, Newbury & Southampton line brought GW locomotives to Eastleigh and Southampton. In 1956, 0-6-0 No 3212 leaves Northam for Southampton Terminus. In the background underneath the skew bridge lies the main line curve to Southampton Central. The lines on the left complete the triangle.

Above:
In the heyday of steam in the 1950s Bulleid Pacifics dominated the main line. Two unrebuilt light Pacifics pose at Bournemouth Central.

train brought a 'Hall' or 'Grange' 4-6-0 from Oxford as part of an arrangement that also took Southern 'Lord Nelsons' and 'King Arthurs' well into WR territory on the northbound service.

There was great excitement in the summer of 1953 when the 'Merchant Navy' 4-6-2s were temporarily withdrawn to have their crank axles tested. To replace them for several weeks came some of the Western Region's unloved 'Britannias', LMS and BR Class 5s from the London Midland Region, and a group of Eastern Region 'V2' 2-6-2s.

In 1956 came the rebuilding of the air-smoothed Bulleid Pacifics into handsome, efficient machines to the designs produced in Ron Jarvis's drawing office at Brighton,

where also had been designed the BR 2-6-4Ts and '9F' 2-10-0s, the SR's contribution to BR's short-lived but excellent standard designs.

During the last days of steam the main line was dominated by the rebuilt Pacifics and many BR standard Class 5s. The older Southern types disappeared as the BR Standard classes arrived. In many cases, following closure of many lines under the Beeching plan, more modern engines including BRCW Type 3 diesels spread west through the Southern to speed the elimination of favourites such as the 'Nelsons', 'Arthurs', 'Schools', the 'T9s', '700s', 'Q1s' and 'M7s'. The last working Maunsell engine I remember seeing there was an 'S15' freight 4-6-0 leaving Eastleigh depot in 1965.

Even the Yankee-tanks, Class USA 0-6-0Ts, were pushed off their established ground at Southampton Docks by Ruston diesel shunters to become, in a few cases, departmental shunters. Other 'USAs' shunted Eastleigh works; some happily received Southern carriage green paint to brighten their last years on BR.

Then came electrification in 1967. A forewarning of what was to come was the use in autumn 1966 of No D6521, the first Sulzer Type 3 to be converted to push-pull (other than the experimental work on D6580), to propel three four-car trailer units (4TCs) on the 11.30 Waterloo-Bournemouth. As more of these units were delivered they were introduced on more rosters. I well remember seeing the down 'Royal Wessex' thunder through Basingstoke early in 1967 after the third rail had gone 'live' all the way. Propelling 12 coaches at about 75mph, the single Class 73 electro-diesel locomotive at the rear drew a huge arc at the west end crossovers — most impressive!

Now, 4REP motor/buffet units (class 430) propel two 4TCs (class 491) to Bournemouth where Class 33/1s take one or two TCs on to Weymouth; the up trains leave Weymouth with the diesel pushing and trains are rejoined at Bournemouth. Most of the TCs, and the trailer coaches in the REPs, were rebuilds of older Mk 1 coaches and are now over 30 years old. If their replacements should come in 1987 or 1988 as is hoped, the REP/TC formations will have run over two million miles each since electrification, providing a fast, regular, reliable service that would have been unbelievable if postulated only a few years before.

Below:
Drummond 'T9s' could still be seen although over 60 years old. No 30287 deputises for a Brighton-based 'West Country' on the Bournemouth-Brighton through train, seen in 1955 stopping at Boscombe.

Looking back, more has gone apart from the steam locomotives. Whole railways have been closed, in the Beeching era, leaving us with only the main lines and the Lymington and Fawley branches. The locomotive depot at Bournemouth is now a car park, and an arterial road runs the length of the site of Bournemouth West station. The Somerset & Dorset disappeared while under Western Region rule, the 'Old Road' from Brockenhurst via Ringwood to Broadstone is no more, and Salisbury no longer has a direct rail link with Bournemouth. The DN&S has gone and the remains of the Alton line survive merely as a preserved steam railway.

The area's fine collection of semaphore signals have all been toppled by colour lights, and track simplification has cut the cost of maintaining the route.

On the positive side, the area's links to the Midlands and the North have been strengthened. Class 47-hauled trains of Mk 2 stock run roughly every two hours via Basingstoke and Reading to such places as Liverpool, Manchester, Glasgow and Birmingham, bringing foreign Regions' locomotives to Bournemouth. While the Lymington boat trains have gone, Bournemouth still performs the locomotive change from diesel-electric to electro-diesel on the Weymouth-Waterloo Channel Islands boat train in summer.

Freight has changed too. The old mixed goods trains hauled sedately by 'S15' 4-6-0s have given way to Freightliners from Southampton's two terminals. So have the Fawley oil trains changed, from '9F' 2-10-0s pulling four-wheeled 45-tonners to pairs of Class 33 diesels on trains of enormous 100-ton bogie tankers.

Most of all I miss the 'Bournemouth Belle'. Everything is now generally faster and more frequent. But the Edwardian elegance of the 'Belle' lives on only in memory.

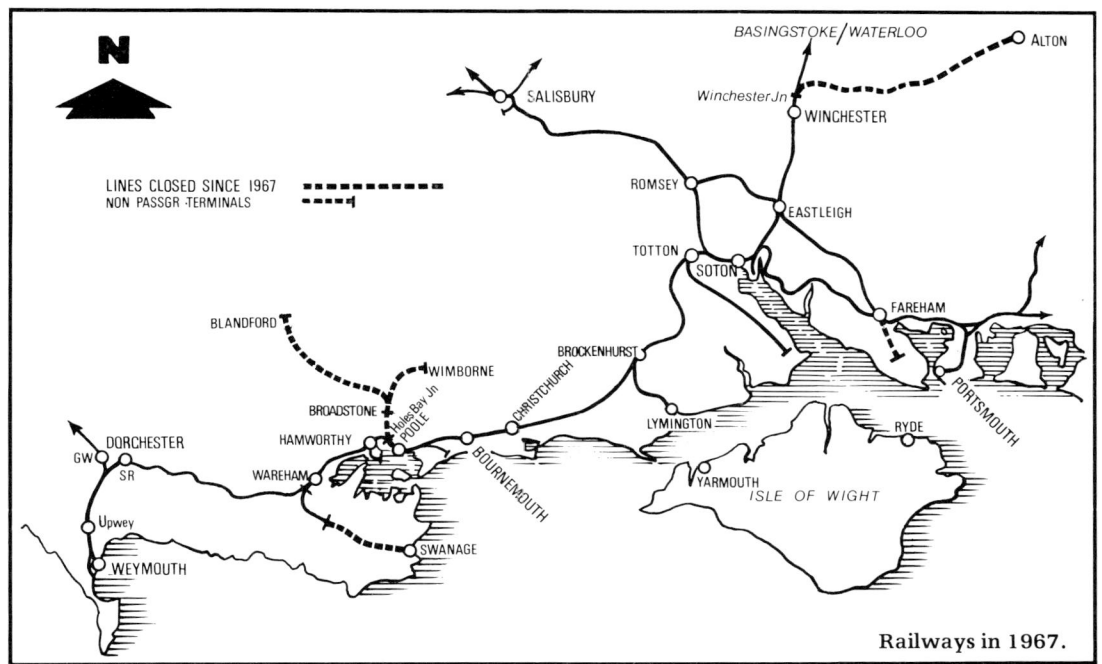

Railways in 1967.

Engines of the big four

Left:
A LMS Class 5 rests in the small shed at Branksome on a Sunday in February 1952 prior to working the next day's 'Pines Express'.

Below:
Ex-GWR 'Hall' class 4-6-0 No 5967 *Bickmarsh Hall* backs into Bournemouth depot after working a Sunday excursion.

Above:
The LNER was unexpectedly represented in the area in 1953 when deputising for temporarily withdrawn 'Merchant Navies'. No 60908 had arrived from Waterloo and was photographed backing into Bournemouth Central's up platform to form the return working.

Above right:
Rebuilding the 'Merchant Navies' was started in 1955. No 35013 *Blue Funnel — certum pete finem* pulls out of Eastleigh with a semi-fast from Bournemouth to Waterloo early in 1956.

The electric look

Below:
Electrification in 1967 brought a revolution in services from London to Southampton and Bournemouth. The 08.47 semi-fast from Waterloo to Bournemouth pauses at Winchester formed by two 4TC sets propelled by a 4REP, all in plain rail blue livery.

Pullman Perfection

It is the departure of the day! At the hour of afternoon tea in Bournemouth's elegant western avenues and roads (Bournemouth only ever had one Street, being otherwise above such mundanity), trolleys of trunks and leather-strapped suitcases are being loaded into the guard's van in the rear Pullman car. A wealthy, portly clientele strolls along Bournemouth West's awned platform. Each passenger confronts a smartly jacketed attendant and is led with competent servility inside one of the 12 Pullman cars.

The interior is predominantly polished mahogany, exquisite marquetry stamping each car with its own unique pattern. Deep, plush carpets and individual chairs greet the first class passenger, while the third class is hardly less comfortable if only a little less spacious. Outside, each vehicle glistens with rich chocolate and cream paint shining deeply through many coats of varnish. Elegant gold lining marks out the panelling. The Pullman name and crests add to the splendour, and each car carries its own name, or at least a number. 'Rosalind', 'Topaz', 'Hibernia' need no endorsement of their class and even a number is not just a number on this train: 'Third class car No 98' in full capital serif script proclaims that third class Pullman is a class above the rest.

As the departure hour of 4.34pm approaches, activity at the front end is intense but controlled. No 35017 *Belgian Marine* stands proud, facing cold almost a mile at 1 in

Above:

In April 1956, newly rebuilt 'Merchant Navy' 4-6-2 No 35018 starts the London-bound Bournemouth Belle out of Bournemouth West. The plume of steam at the rear indicates a helping push from an 'M7' 0-4-4T.

90 with over 480 tons of train behind the tender drawhook. The green flag is waved, and the Pacific quietly eases forward, its steam sanders going full blast beneath the driving wheels. The driver pumps the

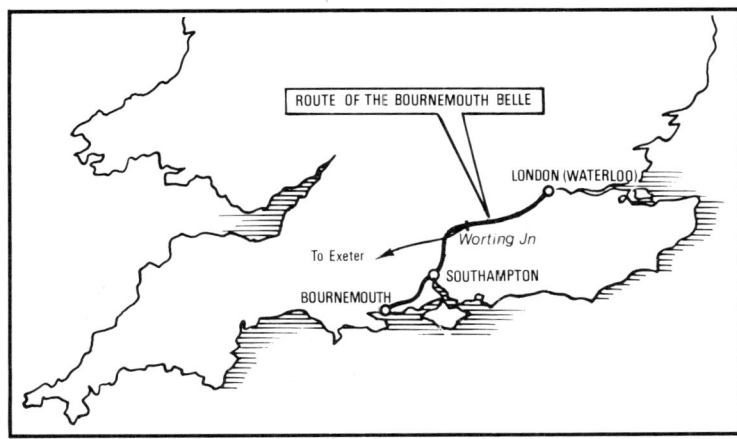

Route of 'Bournemouth Belle'.

regulator handle back and forward at first, to keep that pent-up power within the limit of adhesion, but very soon the soft, sharp, slightly uneven beat of the 'Merchant Navy' is heard climbing steadily past the carriage sheds. The train slips westwards across into the Borough of Poole, and, as if embarrassed by such indiscretion, curves north, back across the red-brick viaduct on the Branksome triangle. Then heading east through pine lined cuttings it bursts through a series of overbridges, passes the engine sheds on the left and stops under the overall roof of Bournemouth Central.

Activity here is far more intense than at the leisurely West terminus. We are due away at 4.45pm and have only three minutes to board most of today's travellers and their luggage.

On time, No 35017 is opened up gently and, with slight wheel slip as she pulls against the long train tight on the curve, the 'Belle' makes to leave Bournemouth on its 108-mile journey to London Waterloo. After a slow start, speed rises rapidly as the train drops to the shallow valley of the rivers Stour and Avon through Christchurch, and then undulates through the New Forest following the curvateous route once known as Castleman's snake by those who contrasted it with the superb alignment of Joseph Locke's London and Southampton railway.

We approach Southampton observing a 'Queen' liner in the dry dock at Millbrook and a mauve-hull 'Castle' ship preparing to leave the New Docks for Cape Town.

Leaving Southampton Central with the tender tank refilled we plunge into Southampton Tunnel, curve past Northam triangle, the link with Terminus station and the old Docks, and head northwards on an uphill grind that is tough, not because of the steepness of its gradients but because of their length. From Eastleigh, where we pass the locomotive and carriage works and two main junctions, there are 16 miles uphill at an unbroken 1 in 252. No 35017 works hard to lift nearly 500 tons of plain-bearing train, gradually steadying at about 55-60mph

through the rolling chalk farmlands above Winchester, while the passengers partake of the excellent and satisfying four-course dinner.

No real breather is possible even after the summit at Roundwood because speed is now of the essence. A long four-track straight stretches ahead from Basingstoke into London's suburbs, and only 75-80mph running can keep us to time.

But after nearly 2hr and 10min the 'Bournemouth Belle' is curving through that ocean of third rails past Vauxhall, and then *Belgian Marine* sighs contentedly as she confronts the long hydraulic buffer stops at Waterloo.

The 'Bournemouth Belle' had first been introduced as an all-Pullman train in 1931, with 'Lord Nelsons' and 'King Arthurs' as power. After the war the train resumed operation in 1946 with Bulleid's new 'Merchant Navy' class in complete command.

Above right:
General Steam Navigation **bursts out of Holdenhurst Road bridge into Bournemouth Central with the down Pullman in April 1956.**

Right:
On Sundays in 1956, Salisbury shed provided engines for the 'Belle'. No 35006 *Peninsular & Oriental SN Co* **enters Bournemouth Central with the up train, passing the engine sheds.**

Above:
The last built 'Merchant Navy', No 35030 *Elder-Dempster Lines*, chunters up through Pokesdown with a commendably clear exhaust in September 1957.

Below:
A flashback to the mid-1930s shows 'Lord Nelson' class 4-6-0 No 862 *Lord Collingwood* making good speed on the down Belle near Farnborough. The experimental Kylchap double chimney may help to date the photograph to near 1934.
Dorset County Libraries

First malachite green, then BR blue with black-and-white lining, and finally Brunswick green, every livery sported by these beefy if expensive machines complemented well the brown-and-cream Pullmans.

The years 1951 to 1954 saw the greatest variety of locomotives ever to be entrusted to the train. 1951 was the year of the Festival of Britain and also marked the introduction of the BR standard Class 7 4-6-2s, the 'Britannias'. The Southern was given two. No 70009 *Alfred the Great* went to Nine Elms depot and performed throughout most of that year on the down and up 'Bournemouth Belle', 12.30pm from Waterloo and 4.34pm return. *Alfred the Great* was an elegant substitute and performed ably.

Then in 1952 the Southern's first two diesel-electric main line locomotives appeared on the route. Nos 10201 and 10202 became regular performers on the 'Belle'. By 1953 a policy decision had put all the BR diesel-electrics together, based at Nine Elms, so Nos 10000 and 10001 joined the ranks of haulers of the Pullman. No 10203, new from Brighton Works, came later.

Then fate struck hard. No 35020 broke its crank axle at speed at Crewkerne, and all 30 'Merchant Navies' were hurriedly withdrawn for testing. Temporary replacements arrived at Nine Elms in the form of Western Region 'Britannias', ER 'V2' 2-6-2s, and BR and LMS Class 5s from the Midland. The 'Belle' was

---

Loco variety

Top left:
New 'Britannia' 4-6-2 No 70009 *Alfred the Great* **worked the 'Bournemouth Belle' roster with great consistency during the summer of 1951.**
Robin Stieber

Centre left:
For a few weeks in 1953, ER 'V2' 2-6-2s were regular performers on the 'Bournemouth Belle', replacing temporarily withdrawn Bulleid Pacifics. No 60896 starts the up Pullman out of Bournemouth Central. *Robin Stieber*

Left:
Diesel traction had a brief fling on the 'Belle' between 1952 and 1954 before all five diesel-electrics were transferred to the London Midland Region. No 10201 is seen at Bournemouth West in August 1954 being coupled to the Pullman.
WHC Kelland collection: Bournemouth Railway Club

'V2' hauled through most of the early summer of 1953. Though dirty and unkempt when they arrived on the Southern, when cleaned by Nine Elms cleaners the 'V2s' looked fine. They were the only black steam engines I ever recall hauling the 'Bournemouth Belle', except one fateful day when No 60893 failed and the 12 Pullmans ended their down journey ignominiously behind Class Q 0-6-0 No 30542.

From 1954 when the diesels went to the west coast main line the 'Belle' returned to 100% steam haulage. Then came the rebuilding of the Bulleid Pacifics, following which the 'Merchant Navies' could be seen starting from Bournemouth Central in a much more sure-footed way. Rebuilt light Pacifics of the 'West Country' and 'Battle of Britain' classes were quite often used as substitutes for their bigger sisters in the later years when the 'Belle' became part of an extensive four-leg roster for Bournemouth based engines.

Dieselisation was only to affect the 'Belle' again for a short time in the mid-1960s. Class 47s became regular power in the last few months of its existence. As electrification meant a standardised, faster, regular interval service, there was no room in the strategy for a Pullman train that only made one journey each way each day.

But when the day came, Sunday 9 July 1967, senior management had decreed no steam haulage, much to the bitter disappointment of the many who had turned out to witness the last runs. No D1924, a respectably clean, green Brush Type 4, performed the last rights that day.

The old 12-wheeled Pullmans that formed the train in the late 1950s and early 1960s had given way to less ancient eight-wheelers when the 'Queen of Scots' Pullman was withdrawn. The preservation movement only really got going in the late 1960s with the result that while many of the eight-wheeled Pullmans are today in use around Britain as restaurants or are on preserved railways, to my imperfect knowledge only one of the grand old 12-wheelers survives.

Of the engines which most regularly hauled the 'Bournemouth Belle', only *Clan Line* and *Lord Nelson* have been steamed in preservation to date, though other Bulleid Pacifics are taking shape at Carnforth, Ropley and Grosmont.

The memorabilium par excellence remains, however. Frank Burridge has the 'Bournemouth Belle' headboard in his Big Four Railway Museum near Horseshoe Common in Bournemouth.

Pacifics and Pullmans

Above:

No 35017 *Belgian Marine* is seen at an impressive angle climbing the 1 in 99 of Pokesdown bank with the down 'Bournemouth Belle' on 1 February 1959.

Below:

The 'Bournemouth Belle' always looked fine in full sunshine. No 35018 thunders through Pokesdown with a train of magnificent 12-wheeled Pullmans in 1956.

Above right:

It was rare for the 'Bournemouth Belle' to be seen west of the Branksome triangle. During a Sunday track possession at New Milton, No 34061 *73 Squadron* had to bring the Pullman via Ringwood. It is seen here at Holes Bay Junction joining the line from Weymouth on 27 March 1960.

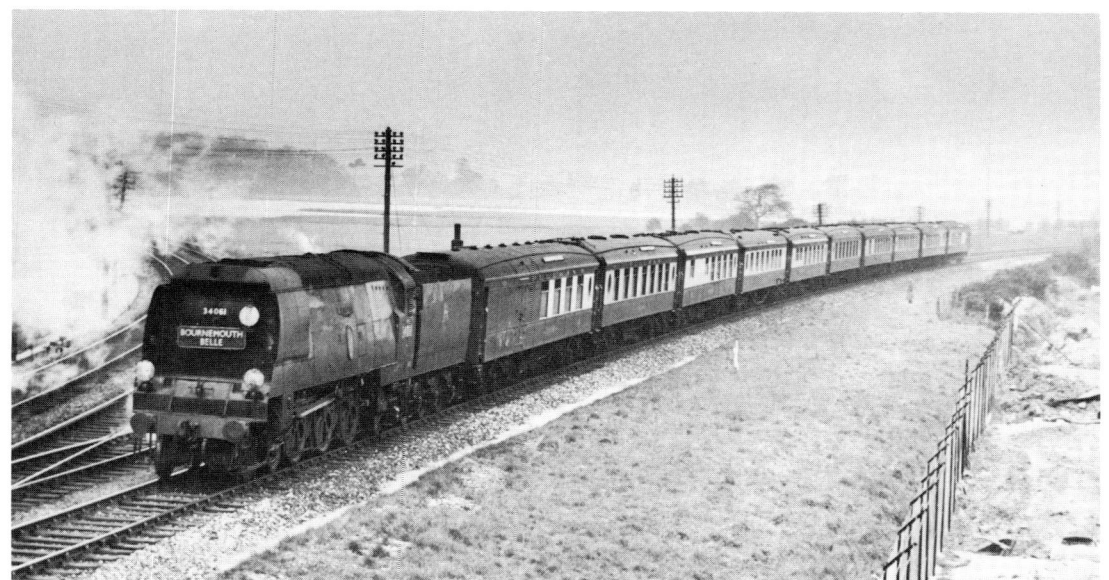

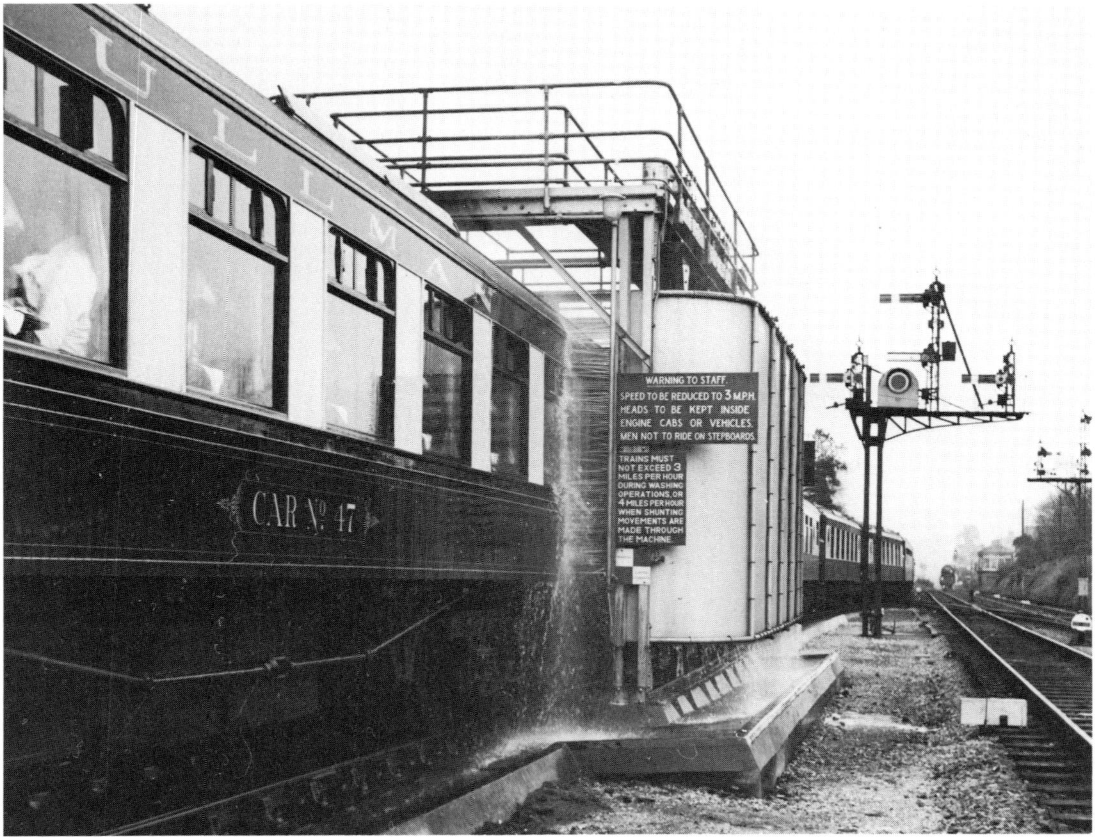

The clean 'Belle'

Above:
The pristine cleanliness of the Pullmans' paintwork was aided by a new carriage washing machine outside Bournemouth West, seen here in March 1957 shortly after commissioning.

The last 'Belle'

Beaulieu Pullman

Above:
Diesel power was again used in the 'Belle's' last year as Eastleigh depot borrowed Brush Type 4s from Cardiff Canton. No D1924 passes through Pokesdown station on the very last down 'Bournemouth Belle' on Sunday 9 July 1967. *John H. Bird*

Below:
No Pullmans were seen on the main line from July 1967 until the summer of 1983 when the newly restored 'Venice-Simplon Orient Express' set was used for some occasional excursions to Brockenhurst for the Beaulieu estate. No 33.029 leans to the curve through Christchurch station with the empty VSOE Pullmans following such a trip on 11 June 1983.

Steam Centre: Bournemouth

There can have been few railway stations in Britain better situated to satisfy the railway enthusiast than the Central station at Bournemouth. At the east end, viewed from the down platform, one had a clear view of up departures. The heavy, steam-hauled London trains frequently caused their locomotives to struggle to gain adhesion, while photographers were happy with the angle of the sun through most of the day.

At the west end of the extended down platform one could sit, protected from all weathers, and watch the workings of the complete motive power depot. Virtually all operations and movements could be observed in comfort, and without trespass!

In between these vantage points was the most impressive overall roofed station west of Waterloo. The roof echoed to the arrivals of Bulleid Pacifics, and to fastidiously detailed loudspeaker announcements. It remains today, though with the glazing substantially

reduced from its former glory. Over the doorway to the up booking office is moulded the date 1885, and the main station buildings remain, at least in outline, much as they were built.

It has always been basically a two-platform through station. In steam days there were two through lines between the two platform tracks. Now only the latter remain. The down platform had its western extension with a scissors crossing adjacent to the signal box. This enabled a full-length main line arrival to be accommodated in the main platform while a Weymouth local could be held in the extension. This facility exists today, but

Below:
The classic view of the east end of Bournemouth Central in 1956 with No 35018 about to depart with the up 'Belle'. The engine carried an Easter weekend train describer number board which partially obscured the headboard.

the through roads have gone, being replaced at the western end by stabling sidings for electric trains.

There is also a short up bay platform which can accommodate a four-car EMU. For many years before electrification this was merely an unnumbered platform used for parcels vans and for stabling locomotives destined to take over up trains.

Operationally the station has always held interest. Formerly every two hours the principal trains from London used to divide here. The front portion went on with the train engine to Weymouth; the rear, usually a complete Bulleid six-car restaurant set, would be taken round to Bournemouth West by whatever engine was available. In the up direction the procedure was more complicated. The restaurant portion from Bournemouth West would arrive first, and the station shunter, 0-4-4T No 30112, or on occasions Nos 30204 or 30318, would couple up to its rear. Once passengers had been boarded the train would be shunted to the long siding immediately adjacent to the engine sheds to await the arrival of the Weymouth portion, usually five to seven mixed coaches headed by the Bulleid Pacific that would take the combined train on to Waterloo. Then the 0-4-4T would awake into action and push the rear portion towards the front. Frequently the buck-eye couplers would fail to engage at the first impact due to the curve, and the resounding clang of colliding couplers would be heard again, sometimes several times.

The Weymouth section was therefore at the front of each up train, as also it was on the down journey. The portions therefore had to be reversed in London, done during layover at Clapham Junction carriage sidings. There was time for such manoeuvres in those days.

In addition to the fasts there were semi-fast trains of 11 to 13 coaches which were worked through from Bournemouth West to Waterloo.

The observer watching operations at the motive power depot had his time full. Engines would arrive off trains, or from the West or from Poole, and enter the depot throat from the connection about midway along the length of the yard, crossing to the headshunt behind the shed, just beyond the observer's gaze. The normal sequence for a locomotive was then to move back on to one of the two coaling roads, where other operations such as watering, smokebox cleaning, ash disposal and boiler blowdown took place. Engines queued for attention from the coaling crane, a tall electric swing-jib, rail-mounted device that discharged bottom-door cubic coal buckets one by one into the waiting tenders.

Loading the buckets was done manually from a row of mineral wagons on the adjacent road. A 'B4' 0-4-0T (old No 93 *St Mclo* was a regular) moved the wagons up one by one as required. The whole thing was quite labour intensive.

Off the coaling road an engine would be balanced on the vacuum driven turntable, and then run across the depot throat once more, to be disposed or stabled on one of the four covered shed roads. Maintenance facilites were available in the shed, with a hoist for lifting just outside.

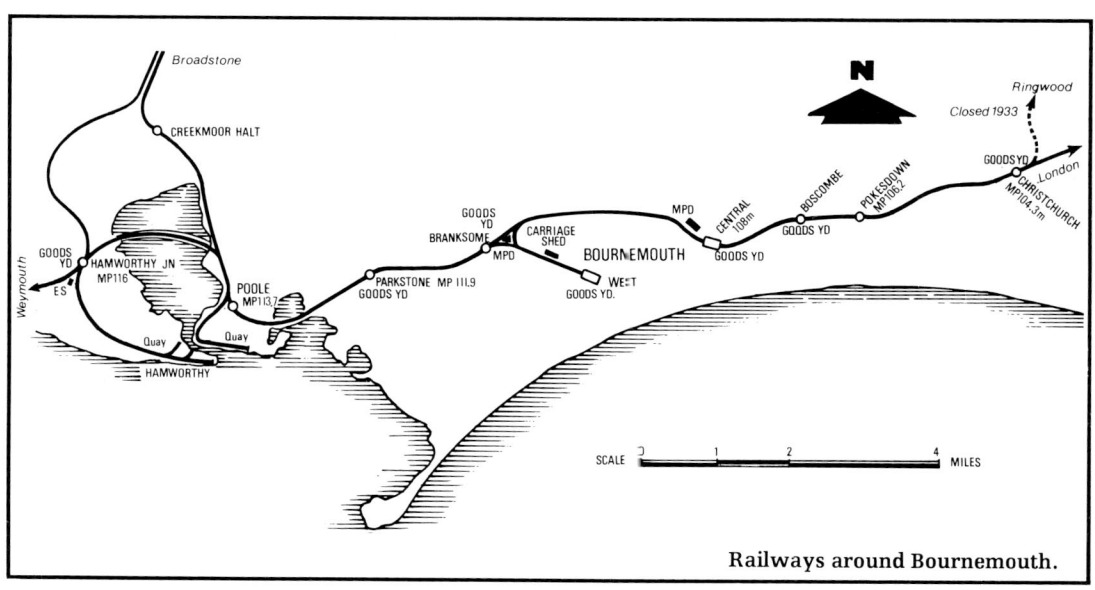

Railways around Bournemouth.

Bournemouth Central possessed only two carriage sidings, infrequently used, beyond the motive power depot.

It did however once boast an active parcels and freight depot on the site of the original Bournemouth East station. This was for many years shunted by Adams Class G6 0-6-0Ts Nos 30260 or 30274, until the Drewry 204hp diesel-mechanical shunters arrived in the mid-1960s.

The first train from London to reach Bournemouth arrived at Bournemouth West in 1874 having come via Ringwood and Wimborne and the link to Holes Bay Junction whence it approached Bournemouth from the west via Poole.

Bournemouth West station had three island platforms, one quite short and two of almost adequate length for main line trains. The main station building, a neat, red-brick gabled structure, flanked one side of the middle island. Long awnings bridged the platform ends and protected the main islands over half their length.

Postwar years saw many heavy trains leave Bournemouth West: Waterloo semifasts, inter-Regional trains via Oxford, and the 'Pines Express' via the Somerset & Dorset. These were in addition to the shorter portions that linked at Central with the Weymouth-Waterloo expresses.

Much of the terminal's activity was with local services. There were the chirpy 'M7' 0-4-4Ts on push-pulls to Brockenhurst via the Old Road, and S&D trains to Templecombe and Bath with Class 5 4-6-0s, '2P' 4-4-0s, '7F' 2-8-0s or '4F' 0-6-0s. There were various Drummond 4-4-0s and standard or SR 2-6-0s on stopping trains to Salisbury or Southampton.

Thus, although it was a relatively quiet terminus, Bournemouth West's motive power variety was extensive. Because most trains apart from Weymouth locals terminated there, the carriage servicing shed was located nearby, half a mile up the incline towards Branksome. At the top of the incline was Branksome triangle where routes connected to the West and Central stations and to Poole and beyond.

Branksome shed lay in this triangle, a small, two-road affair with a turntable and very little else. Any top-up coaling was manual. The shed was host largely to locomotives from the Somerset & Dorset line, mainly LMS or BR standard types. A regular Southern visitor, however, was the 'Merchant Navy' off the 'Bournemouth Belle' which turned on the triangle and was watered at

Top:
Under the cavernous roof of Bournemouth Central station, 'U' 2-6-0 No 31802, one of the ex-'River' class 2-6-4T conversions, stables stock in one of the centre through roads. The photograph shows the condition of the station in February 1957.

Above:
Coal for Bournemouth depot is lifted from the station through track by standard 2-6-0 No 76022. In the foreground is the Central station down platform and its scissors crossing. The signal is off for a BR standard 4-6-0 to back light to Bournemouth West to join an up train. Photographed in 1964. *Alan Thorpe*

Branksome to avoid the delay involved in getting to and from Bournemouth depot in view of the limited turnround time.

As the years progressed and the branches withered an end-of-town terminus had less relevance to modern life. Bournemouth

Central prospered. Bournemouth West closed in 1966, one of only two stations to close between Waterloo and Bournemouth. On the site of the main line near Branksome triangle is now an EMU maintenance depot. The station site is occupied by a main road; no-one would know now that a railway had once sprung from that spot.

Electrification came to Bournemouth in 1967. Operationally it remains interesting because trains still divide at Bournemouth station. Weymouth portions are entrusted to diesel traction, but as the West station is no more the Bournemouth portions just stable or are turned back.

Above:
Bournemouth Central's down platform extension was the base from which railway enthusiasts watched operations. No 73116 arrives past the engine sheds with the 9.25am from Weymouth on 7 April 1956.

Below left:
In 1953, 1Co-Co1 diesel-electric No 10201 arrives at Bournemouth Central with the 2.30pm from Bournemouth West to Waterloo.

The mode of operation is unique in the UK. From Waterloo the service frequency is virtually double that of the years of steam. Hourly expresses (always announced as Inter-City) leave Waterloo at 35min past each hour, stopping only at Southampton. These are formed by a four-car class 430 (4REP) tractor-buffet unit at the rear, propelling two Class 491 trailer (4TC) sets. At Bournemouth a Class 33/1 diesel electric backs on the front of the train and takes one or two trailer sets on to Weymouth. The 4REP plus a 4TC if one remains crosses to the up platform to form the next up fast working, and awaits its Weymouth portion which arrives as a push-pull, Class 33/1 at the rear.

Also each hour a similar 12-car formation leaves Waterloo 10min behind the fast,

forming a semi-fast service to Bournemouth only, calling at eight intermediate stations.

Over the years the journey times have been speeded up. The fasts now complete the 108 miles to Bournemouth in 98min, while the semi-fasts take 126. (Steam trains took 120 and about 155min respectively.) Hourly stopping trains are formed of Class 423 (4VEP) units.

Thus the rationalised Bournemouth station has a service of nearly twice the capacity of that provided in steam days. It is now quiet, clean and a highly successful passenger terminal. Formerly it was noisy, steam timekeeping was erratic, and we enthusiasts came home grubby — the price to pay for the excitement of steam!

Yard freight

Right:
The daily coal empties from Bournemouth shed to the East Yard were photographed in February 1957 climbing the 1 in 150 out of Central station behind 'N15' 4-6-0 No 30783 *Sir Gillemere.*

Below:
Adams 'G6' 0-6-0T No 30260 was a regular engine for the East Yard shunt, and was so doing on 16 February 1957.

Summer visitor

Bournemouth West

Above:
Adding to the power variety on occasions were the Remembrance 4-6-0s from Nine Elms. No 32329 *Stephenson* starts the 3.55pm to Waterloo out of Bournemouth Central on 7 August 1955.

Below:
A rare 1954 interior view of Bournemouth West, showing standard '5' No 73051 having arrived with a train from the north via the Somerset & Dorset line. 'West Country' 34043 *Combe Martin* is arriving with what could be the Birkenhead-Bournemouth through train

Top:
A Class 7F 2-8-0 from the S&D (note tablet catcher on the tender side) arrives at the West station with a Saturday extra from the north in 1955.

Above:
'02s' and 'M7s' were used to shunt Bournemouth West. '02' 0-4-4T No 30177 was photographed on this duty in 1954. *Alan Trickett*

Left:
Up the bank from Bournemouth West were the carriage sidings. 'M7' No 30060 is passing with the 2.8pm push-pull from Brockenhurst via the Old Road on 30 August 1958. *K. L. Cook*

Boscombe

Modern times

Left:
The quite substantial station at Boscombe was closed in the early 1960s and largely demolished. LM-designed 2-6-4T No 42096 is an unusual visitor on the 3.54pm from Bournemouth Central to Andover on 11 April 1955.

Below left:
This 1979 view of Bournemouth Central shows how much has changed since the photograph on page 25 was taken. On the left, an up Weymouth push-pull set approaches a 4REP which will haul it to Waterloo. On the right a 12-car TC/TC/REP formation has arrived on a semi-fast working.

Below:
Electro-diesel No 73.119 has taken over the up Weymouth-Waterloo Channel Islands boat train from a Class 33. The stark appearance of Bournemouth station in 1983 compared with former years is evident.

Steam Centre: Southampton

To many world-wide travellers the gates to Southampton Docks represented the gateway to the world, the start of an adventure.

To a party of youngsters from the Bournemouth Railway Club visiting the Docks for the first time, it was an adventure. Our permit bade us report to the gate near the Ocean Terminal. Beyond was a myriad of assorted oblong docks flanked by rail-fed warehouses, some of enormous length. The target of our interest was the group of 14 ex-US Army 0-6-0Ts whose territory this was. Chunky, very strong little beasts were these, whose short wheelbases gave them right of way over almost the whole intricate network of lines.

Each engine's cab roof sported an aerial, a tell-tale sign that operations in such a vast area were under tight radio control. Home base for the locomotives was a small shed in the Old Docks. In addition to the Yankee-tanks, and some Eastleigh-based 'B4' dock tanks, were a couple of ex-London, Brighton & South Coast Railway Class E1 0-6-0Ts. These tended to keep to the transfer freights between the Old and New Docks.

To reach the New Docks a freight had to leave the Old Docks at the western end, proceed alongside a town street, pass the Southampton Town Quay (of which more later) and run another $\frac{1}{2}$-mile to reach the easternmost gate of the New Docks, now known as the Western Docks. Whereas the Old Docks were a hung-together collection of docks and basins, the New stretched for nearly three miles on the continuous straight side of Southampton Water. From here, the Union Castle liners would leave weekly for South Africa. Special boat trains reached them via the Millbrook gate. A very heavy trade was in bananas: long trains of fitted vans, usually 'S15'-hauled, regularly steamed away from these railway-owned docks, each wagon labelled Fyffes to proclaim its contents.

Among all this activity the 'USA' tanks competently served all quays — except one.

Southampton Town Quay was at right angles to the inter-docks transfer railway and was approached round a very sharp curve. This was the domain of Eastleigh depot's most diminutive engines, one of which was here each day. The Class C14 0-4-0Ts started life as 2-2-0T motor train engines but were subsequently converted to shunting tanks in which form they were ideal for lightly laid, tortuous sidings.

Docks shunters

Above:
A typical Docks scene in 1955 as two 'USA' 0-6-0Ts pause between duties. A cruise liner graces the background.

Left:
The 'USA' tanks were replaced in 1962 by Ruston/ Paxman 275hp 0-6-0 diesel-electrics like No D2992, seen here at Eastleigh in 1969 after being displaced in its turn by the decline in docks rail traffic.

Another 'C14', in service stock as No 77s, used to work in the Chief Civil Engineer's works at Redbridge. This also subsequently found its way to the Town Quay where it ended its career.

It is hard to realise that, despite the confidence shown in the future of the Docks' railways by the purchase in 1962 of 14 Ruston 275hp 0-6-0 diesel-electrics as successors to the Yankee-tanks, little over 15 years later the rôle of rail in the Western and Eastern Docks had collapsed, to be replaced by the new containerport beyond Millbrook, now effectively served by *two* Freightliner depots.

My college days were in Southampton. Lunchtimes were frequently spent watching operations at Southampton Central, a compact four-platform station with one west end bay. The lunchtime star was the through Brighton-Plymouth train which, though rostered for a 'West Country', would sometimes appear behind a three-cylinder 'U1' 2-6-0 or even a BR standard 2-6-4T. This train was often followed by a long, local freight bound for Fawley, usually hauled by a new BR Class 3 2-6-2T.

Or one's lunch sandwiches were partaken at Northam, a since-disappeared station on the Terminus leg of the triangle just east of Southampton Tunnel. A GW 2-6-0 or 0-6-0 appeared at this time with a train from Newbury to Southampton Terminus. One fine day this duty was given to the newly restored 4-4-0 No 3440 *City of Truro*. That sight took a lot of believing at the time!

Southampton Terminus was the original terminus of the London & Southampton Railway and was sited close to the docks, quite a way from the city centre which tended to grow in a northerly direction away from the Terminus. After the opening of Southampton West (later renamed Central) the Terminus became the quiet starting point of local services to destinations such as Bournemouth, Alton, Eastleigh, Salisbury and to the Didcot, Newbury & Southampton line.

Even when dieselisation began in 1959, the hourly Alton DEMU service started here. We didn't spend much of our lunch-hour observation time at the Terminus, however. The mixture of Moguls, 'T9s' and the occasional GW engines was not enough to hold our interest. Nor that, it seemed, of BR as the Terminus and Northam succumbed to the Beeching axe.

Town Quay

Below:
Class E1 0-6-0T No 32689 trundles a transfer freight between the Old and New Docks and passes Southampton Town Quay on 25 October 1955.

Above right:
One of the 'C14' class 0-4-0Ts used at Southampton Town Quay was No 77s, formerly at the Redbridge CCE works. Its short wheelbase and overhang were ideal for the sharp curves there.

From the Containerport

Below:
Freight from Southampton Docks is now virtually all in containers. A Freightliner train from one of the Millbrook terminals approaches Southampton Tunnel behind Class 47 No 1919 in 1969.

Steam at Central

Above left:
A flashback to when Southampton Central was the West station and had an up signalbox and east end footbridge. Somewhere between 1926 and 1934 an Adams 4-4-0 pilots a 'King Arthur' on an evening up service. *Hampshire County Libraries*

Left:
No 30457 *Sir Bedivere* pauses at Southampton Central in 1955 with an up Bournemouth line train.

Above:
No 35018 awaits departure from Southampton Central with a Waterloo-Bournemouth express in March 1956.

Right:
Electrification brought with it a new office block in place of Central station's beloved clock tower. An up semi-fast pauses alongside a DEMU for Portsmouth in August 1968.

East of the tunnel

Above:
One of Urie's heavy mixed traffic 'H15' 4-6-0s, No 30490, hurries an up stopping train along the main line between Millbrook and Southampton Central in 1955.

Below:
Three 'T9' 4-4-0s at Southampton Terminus station are dwarfed by the *Queen Mary* and *Queen Elizabeth* Cunard liners in the background. Photographed on 1 May 1956.

Left:
Northam station was a casualty to closure in the early 1960s. In 1956, Churchward 2-6-0 No 5330 enters the station with a train from Didcot via the DN&S line.

Below:
No 3440 *City of Truro* was a surprise resurrection in 1957, seen here on an up DN&S working.

Bottom:
Tunnel Junction at Southampton. No 35017 *Belgian Marine* leans to the curve on the 8.53am Bournemouth to Waterloo on 13 September 1964. The link to the Terminus curves off to the left of this scene. *Michael J. Fox*

In L&SWR days

Above:
Probably just after World War 1, 'B4' 0-4-0T No 91 crosses Canute Road with cattle wagons from the docks. *Hampshire County Libraries*

Railways around Southampton and Eastleigh.

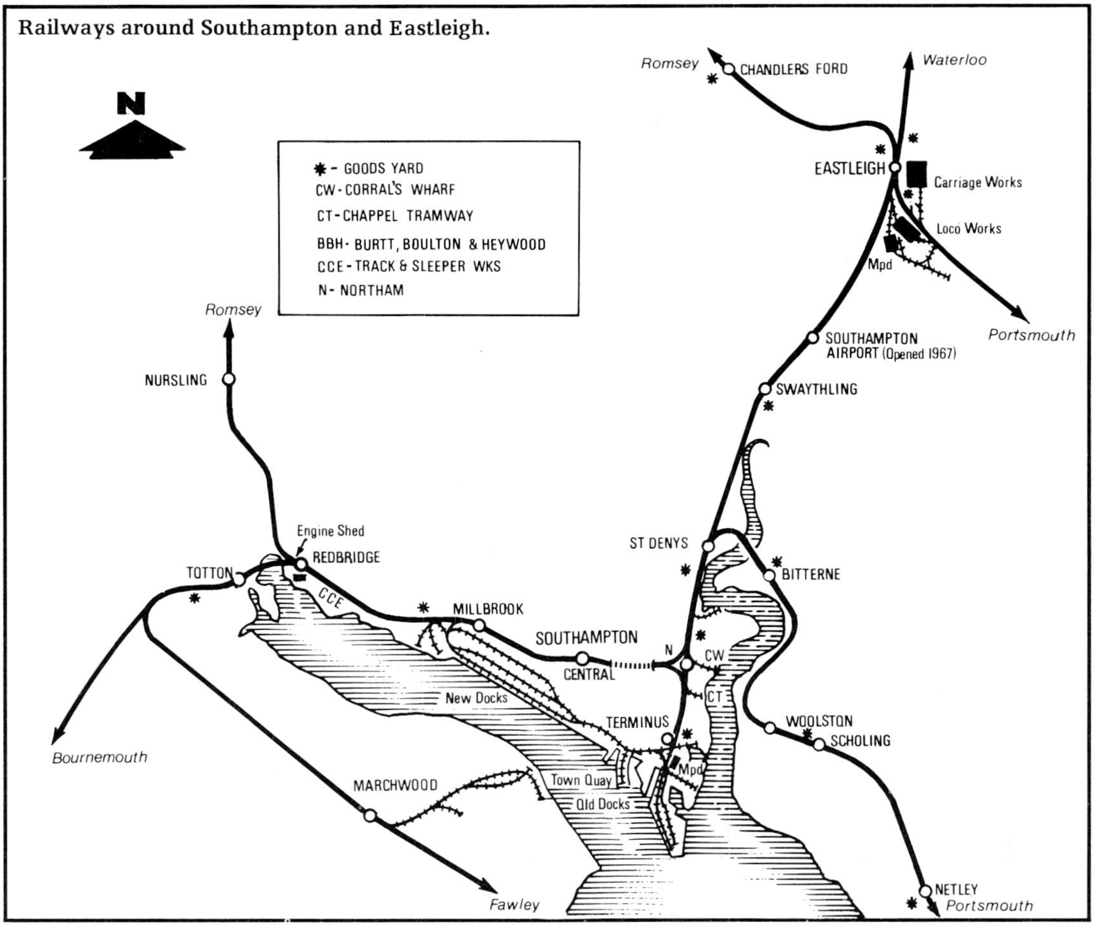

N

* – GOODS YARD
CW – CORRAL'S WHARF
CT – CHAPPEL TRAMWAY
BBH – BURTT, BOULTON & HEYWOOD
CCE – TRACK & SLEEPER WKS
N – NORTHAM

Romsey CHANDLERS FORD *Waterloo*

EASTLEIGH
Carriage Works
Loco Works
Mpd
Portsmouth

SOUTHAMPTON AIRPORT (Opened 1967)

SWAYTHLING

Romsey

NURSLING

Engine Shed
REDBRIDGE

ST DENYS
BITTERNE

TOTTON
CCE

MILLBROOK

SOUTHAMPTON CENTRAL

N
CW
CT

New Docks

Bournemouth

TERMINUS

WOOLSTON
SCHOLING

MARCHWOOD

Town Quay
Old Docks

Mpd

NETLEY
Portsmouth

Fawley

40

Steam Centre: Eastleigh

Not only is Eastleigh a main station on the Waterloo-Bournemouth main line but the town looms large in the author's life as the place where he started his railway career.

'It's damned hard work, but an excellent grounding for a young engineer', so said K. H. Morriss, Works Manager at the locomotive works, at my interview. To a 16-year old it was an awe-inspiring place — the erecting shop with its overhead cranes carrying a locomotive along the shop, the iron foundry a-fog with fumes as the cupola was lit up on a Monday morning, the chattering and clatter of machines, the earth-shaking thump of the huge steam hammers in the forge, the ear-shattering riveting among the boilers. Such a place breeds tough people, quite different from the more gentlemanly crowd in the carriage works next door, a crowd I worked with many years later in my career. Yet if anything the activity rate was higher in the carriage works in those days, so demanding was the 'conveyor belt' atmosphere of the progressive system that forced all coaches along the production line.

These two great works between them employed over 3,000 people and were the heart of the town of Eastleigh. The railway had spawned the town when it moved its works from Nine Elms at the start of the century. The works and the town deserve a book to themselves.

No less an exciting place was the large motive power depot which in its heyday housed up to 140 steam locomotives, providing power for services from both Southampton and Eastleigh. (Southampton was unusual among large cities in not having a main line locomotive depot.) Eastleigh's pride were its 'Lord Nelson' 4-6-0s, but most Southern and ex-LSW types were seen here as they came and went when works overhauls were due. By all standards Eastleigh shed was a very large depot. Engines arrived on a dedicated double track approach (one in, one out). A driver would book his engine's arrival at the hut before the turntable, then proceed, turned if necessary, to the coaling stage. This was a two-storey, red-brick affair. Coal reached it in wagons shunted up an inclined embankment and was manually unloaded into tip-skips for discharge into the tenders waiting below.

After coaling, a locomotive would move to the shunt neck, or even round the triangle if not otherwise turned, and then back into one of the washout roads in the shed.

Part of my apprenticeship was at this depot, learning the art of running maintenance. I even worked on diesels for the first time here — on the 350hp Ashford-built shunters that had ousted the 'Z' class 0-8-0Ts from their posts in the yards at Eastleigh and Allbrook.

The station at Eastleigh was excellent for observing traffic. There were, and are, four platform faces on two islands, up local, up main loop, down main loop and down local, with the up and down fast lines passing through the middle. In steam days the main line was limited to 85mph and this applied right through Eastleigh on the fast lines. To see a Bulleid Pacific on a down express, bucking across the junctions at the north end of the station was quite thrilling.

Almost as exciting was the succession of very heavy freights that thundered through behind 4-6-0s of the 'S15' and 'H15' types. Most of these emanated from Southampton, either the Docks or Bevois Park yard near St Denys.

Since electrification of the main line in 1967 the traffic pattern has remained stable, except for the elimination of general freight from the docks and its replacement by Freightliners. Significant freight expansion has occurred in the fields of cement, oil from Fawley, aggregates and motor cars.

Also in 1967 the carriage works was physically merged with the locomotive works. The former carriage works buildings are now an industrial estate, and the present, combined works meets the needs of the Southern Region with a progressive carriage repair layout that is the envy of several other main works.

At the elimination of steam, all withdrawn engines were hauled for immediate storage at either Salisbury or Weymouth. A new diesel maintenance shed was already well established near the old steam depot. Demolition of the steam shed made room for an array of stock storage sidings. Thus ended steam at Eastleigh.

Eastleigh Works and products

Above:
The locomotive works at Eastleigh in April 1960 showing, left to right, the main erecting shop building, the fitting and machine shop bays, and the separate foundry block.

Below:
Locomotives in varying stages of repair in Eastleigh's erecting shop in 1960.

Right:
A newly rebuilt 'West Country' is lifted on to its coupled wheels by two 50 ton overhead cranes.

43

Left:
No 34016 *Bodmin* waits outside Eastleigh locomotive works for its new phase of life as a rebuilt 'West Country' to begin, in March 1959.

Centre left:
An old-timer after general overhaul, 1874-built Beattie well-tank No 30586 from Wadebridge, waits to return to the far west early in 1959.

Bottom left:
After the carriage works had been absorbed into the locomotive works site, 'Brighton Belle' five-car Pullman electric unit No 3053 awaits its delivery run to London, Wimbledon. This was in 1969.

Right:
The carriage works departmental shunting locomotive was this Fowler 0-4-0 diesel-mechanical No 600s.

Trains around Eastleigh

Above:
A heavy freight hauled by 'S15' 4-6-0 No 30500 thunders through Eastleigh station en route to Southampton early in July 1955.

Below:
While No 35027 *Port Line* leaves Eastleigh on a down semi-fast, Ivatt 2-6-2T No 41304 arrives on a Southampton to Alton service in July 1955.

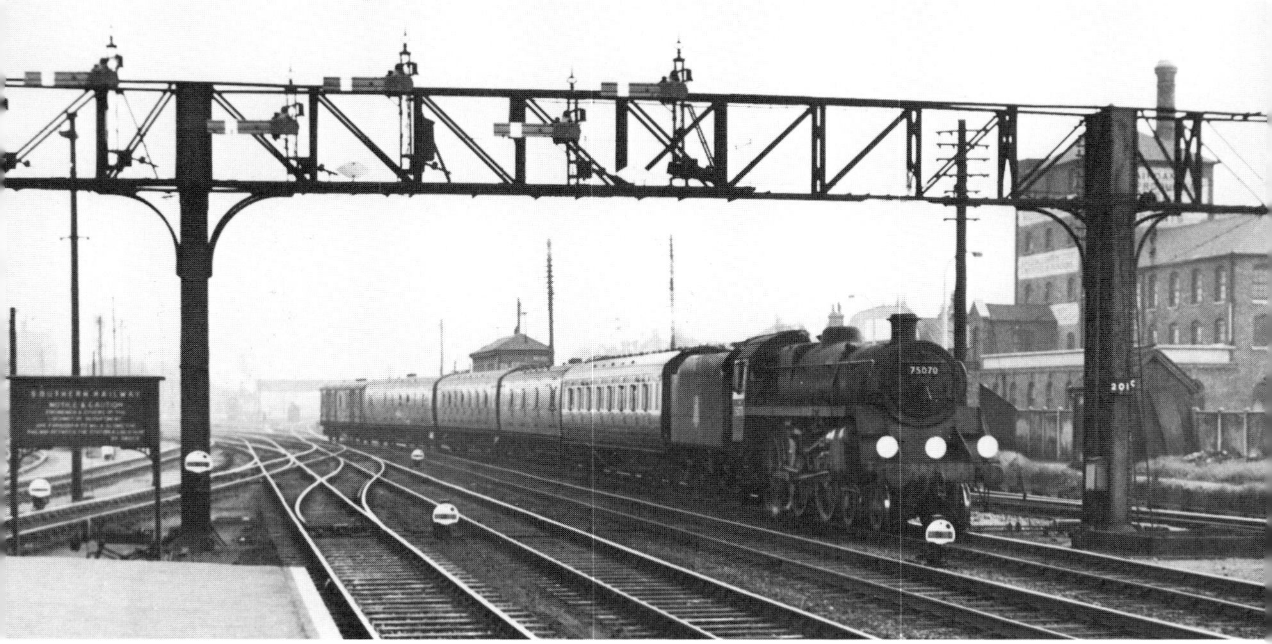
SOUTHERN RAILWAY
75070
201

SPL
21

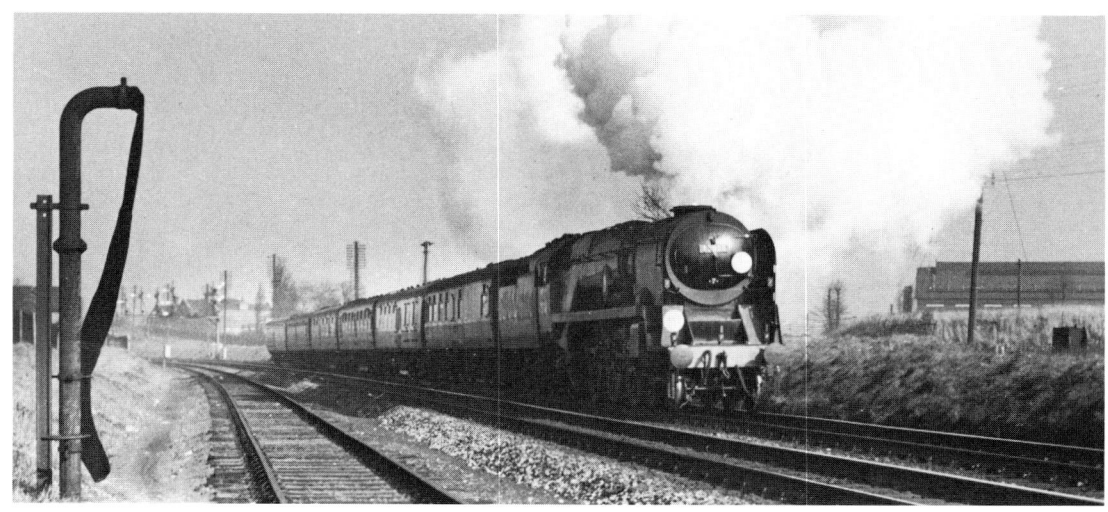

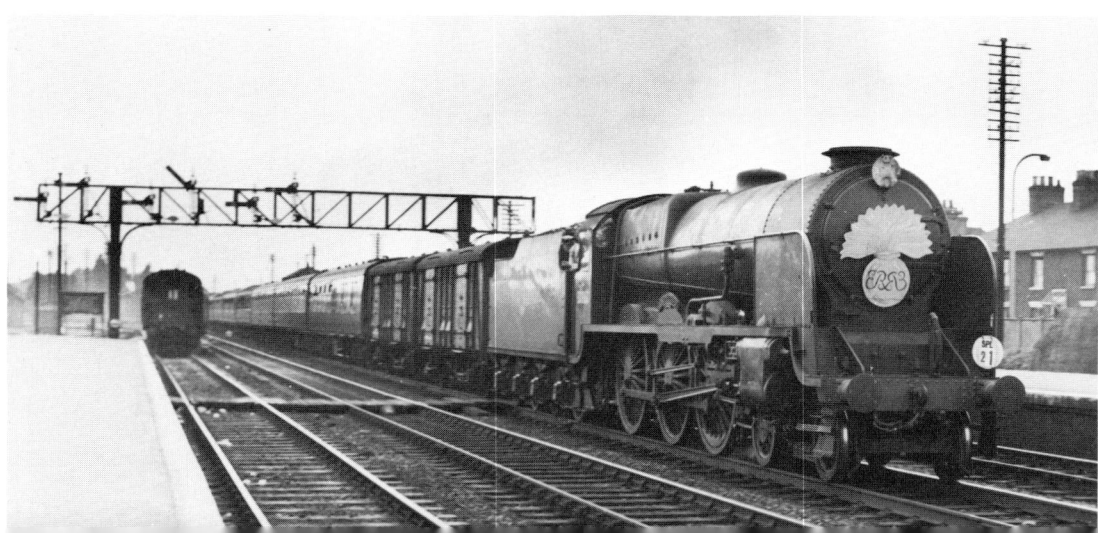

Left:
No 75070 comes off the Portsmouth line with a stopping train on 22 May 1956.

Centre left:
The 12.23pm stopping train from Eastleigh to Southampton which later continued to Bournemouth was a favourite turn for running-in ex-works engines. Newly rebuilt *Holland-Afrika Line* was on this train on 20 February 1957. The water column (left) was a wartime relic serving a group of disused up holding sidings.

Bottom left:
No 30863 *Lord Rodney* rushes through Eastleigh on an up troop train from Southampton Docks on 8 August 1959.

Right:
Freight for the Salisbury line leaves Eastleigh behind 'H15' (rebuilt from Drummond 'F13') 4-6-0 No 30333.

Below:
In August 1968, short-lived large electro-diesel Bo-Bo No E6104 takes the 10.30 Waterloo-Bournemouth through Eastleigh station.

Wessex Artery

It was my pleasure one day around 1960 to introduce the Bournemouth main line to a friend from Eastleigh. We joined the through train from Newcastle, which had rolled into Eastleigh rather unusually behind a BR Class 4 4-6-0 instead of the then more usual SR 4-6-0 of power Class 5.

The few flat miles to Southampton presented no problem, and we swung through Northam Junction at the regulation 15mph to enter Southampton Tunnel before stopping at Southampton Central.

Having a smaller than usual engine on 12 coaches usually highlighted the difficult parts of a route, and this was no exception. Our

Below:

The notorious Northam curve was the beginning of the western extension of the railway towards Dorchester. 'Scotch Arthur' No 30765 *Sir Gareth* **rounds the curve with the 8.37am from Newcastle to Bournemouth on 2 August 1957.**

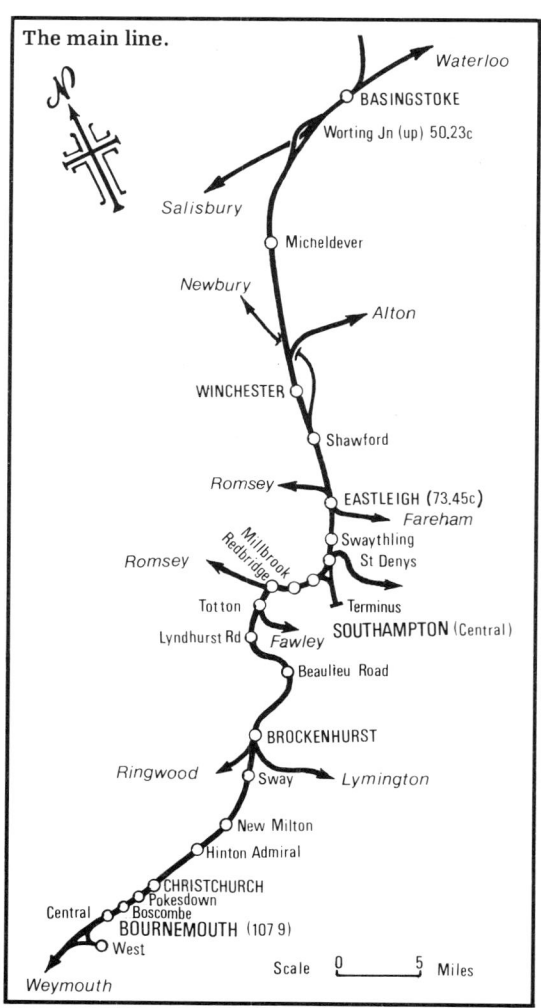

The main line.

driver was determined to extract Class 5 performance from his Class 4! We roared out of Southampton past the New Docks, slackened off to 40mph for the causeway across the end of Southampton Water and at Totton the engine was opened out in earnest. As the Fawley branch disappeared into the trees on the left, our 4-6-0's sharp exhaust echoed off the bungalows of the growing suburb of Ashurst. We leaned to the curve as we entered the New Forest at Lyndhurst Road.

While it contains many trees and woods, the predominant New Forest landscape is gorse-covered heathland, the grazing ground of hundreds of wild ponies. The lonely Beaulieu Road station (why is it pronounced Bewly?) lies at a railway summit in the midst of such a heath, whence the line heads through a cutting, and down into the woods at Woodfidley. No deer could be seen on this occasion. There it curves through a 75mph restriction that offers impediment to electric progress today but which was of no concern to our 65mph 4-6-0!

North of Eastleigh

Above right:
Class V 'Schools' 4-4-0 No 30902 *Wellington* **hurries a Waterloo-Lymington boat train down the main line near Basingstoke on 18 August 1962.** *Alan Trickett*

Right:
Oil from the Esso refinery at Fawley is speeded northwards to Bromford Bridge by '9F' 2-10-0 No 92211, seen near Allbrook on 17 March 1963.

Below:
The echoes of Winchester are raised by Standard '5' 4-6-0 No 73110 *The Red Knight* **on the up** *Canberra* **boat train from Southampton Docks to Waterloo on 11 August 1962.**

'S15' 4-6-0 No 30502 struggles past Allbrook with an up heavy freight to Feltham in March 1963.

It is a feature of this end of the Bournemouth line that principal stations, and speed restrictions, occur at the feet of steep inclines. This prevents high-speed running and impedes restarts. Brockenhurst is no exception. The train approaches along what could otherwise be a racing track, rattles across the town centre's level crossing, and stops at a surprisingly large four-platform station.

Here the station announcer would intone, 'Change here for Lymington and the Isle of Wight; Holmsley, Ringwood and the Wimborne line'.

Like our steam locomotive, the Ringwood line has long since disappeared.

My friend was now to be very impressed indeed by the display of energy from the 4-6-0. Just beyond Brockenhurst the two branches peeled off either side of the main line and we attacked the sharp climb to Sway and out of the New Forest. Our Class 4 4-6-0 hammered hard across the heath, roared through Sway station and accelerated on the undulating line that passes in a cutting between the well-heeled houses of these parts. First New Milton flashed past, then we began to drop steeply from milepost 100 and speeded ever faster through Hinton Admiral station and out on to that long embankment that always spells for me — 'nearly home'.

Again, on a descending track on a reducing embankment over a flat, alluvial, farmland plain we have the recipe for a racetrack, and indeed even in steam days few trains failed to top 70mph here. But right at the bottom comes the 60mph restriction through the reverse curves at Christchurch, and the line enters Bournemouth with two miles of 1 in 99 to surmount. Our Class 4's exhaust crackled effectively as we passed a myriad of small detached houses as far as the eye could see, until we flogged through a short cutting and burst under the road bridge into Pokesdown station. The onslaught on one's ears continued as the 4-6-0 breasted the climb and accelerated briefly through the since-closed station at Boscombe before coasting past more houses, past the goods yard flanked by the Corporation depot with its yellow trolley-buses, and down into another cutting, under Holdenhurst Road bridge and round the curve into Bournemouth Central.

Truly, the nickname of 'Castleman's snake' is an apt description for such a railway. It is quite different to Joseph Locke's superbly engineered London & Southampton Railway.

My friend now knew that railways in the south of England are not flat! But he had yet to see the one with the *real* gradients. Our trip to the Somerset & Dorset was to come later!

Through Eastleigh and Southampton

Above:
No 30857 *Lord Howe* speeds through Eastleigh
with the 11.30am from Waterloo to Bournemouth.
The two tracks in the foreground are the
locomotive depot access roads.

Left:
A popular evening down train was the 'Royal
Wessex', 4.35pm from Waterloo with portions for
Bournemouth West, Swanage and Weymouth.
No 35021 *New Zealand Line* passes Eastleigh
airport with the train on 9 September 1959.

Below left:
One wonders just how many pigeons are carried in
the 15 bogie vans heading out of Southampton
towards Millbrook behind 2-10-0 No 92205!
Photographed in May 1963.　*Roy Panting*

Near Bournemouth

Above:
The truncated remains of the former branch from Ringwood are visible on the left as Urie 'N15' No 30742 *Camelot* approaches Christchurch with a stopping train from Southampton to Bournemouth on 9 April 1955.

Left:
No 35022 *Holland-America Line* tackles the 1 in 99 towards Pokesdown at dusk on 8 September 1956 with the down 'Royal Wessex'.

Below left:
Accelerating through Boscombe is No 35022 on the 10.40am from Bournemouth Central to Waterloo in February 1957.

Top right:
Pokesdown was a later station to be built and shows its Southern Railway lineage with the concrete lift towers. *Brocklebank Line* runs through with the 10.40am Bournemouth-Waterloo.

Right:
Among the pines, 'King Arthur' No 30764 *Sir Gawain* approaches Bournemouth Central with the up through train to York on 22 September 1956.

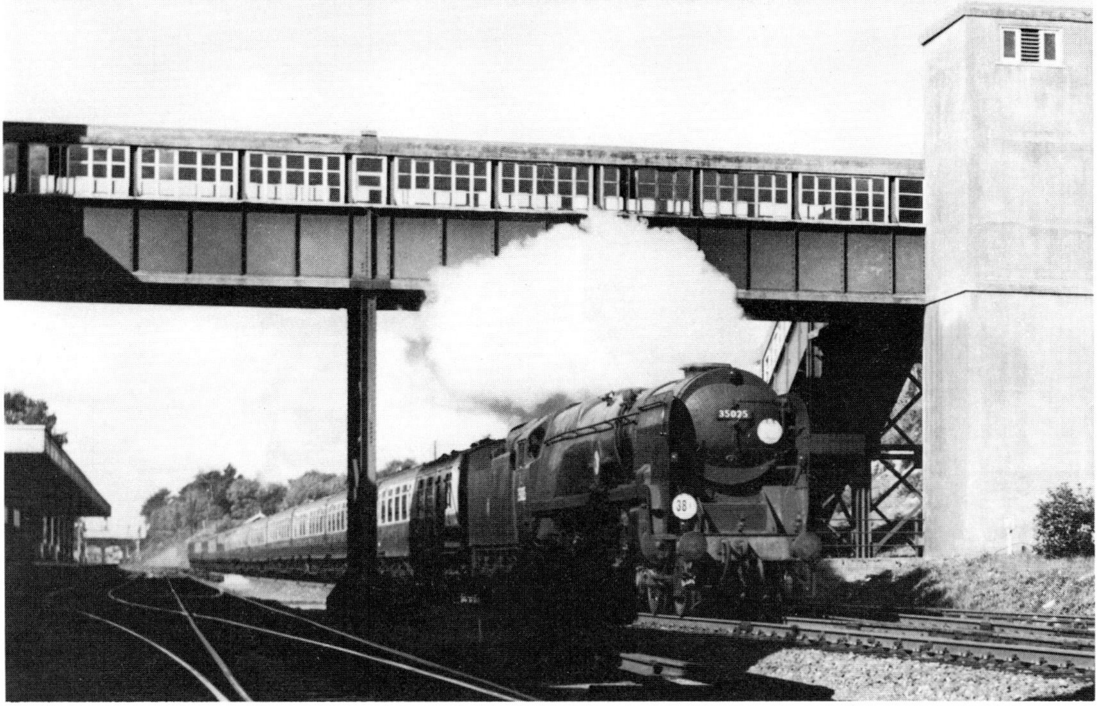
35025

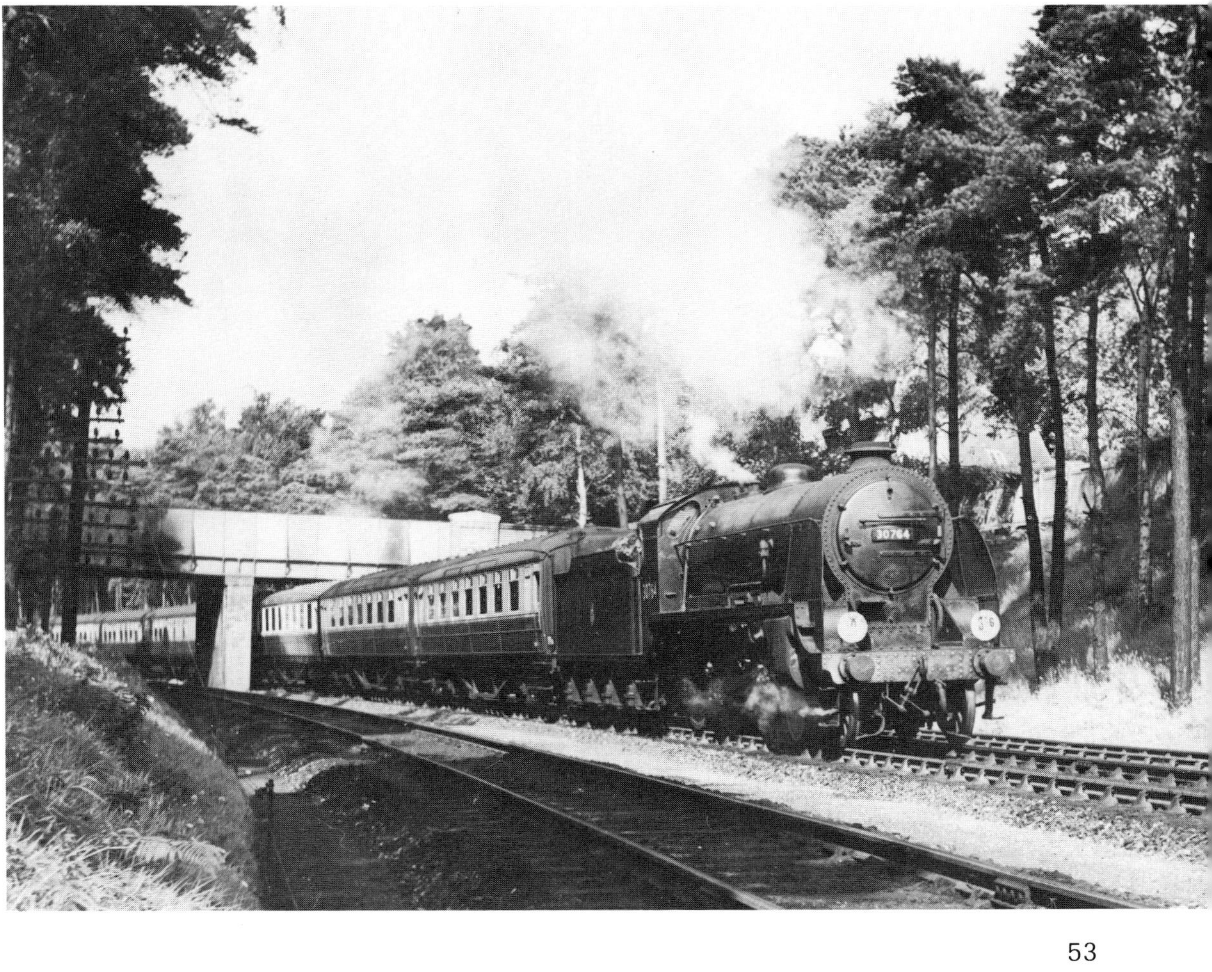
30764

Light light engine

Diesel no more

Above:
No 30087, a 'B4' dock tank on its way to take up duties in Southampton docks, looks dwarfed by the signal gantry as it waddles down the main line just outside Eastleigh.

Below:
After steam had gone, inter-Regional freights had Western Region diesel-hydraulics or LM Brush 4s, as well as Southern Type 3s. Since also displaced, 'Hymek' No D7049 approaches the then new Southampton Airport station with northbound empties in August 1968.

Dorsetway

In the old days Weymouth was Great Western. Little boys from Bournemouth used to go there to spot engines from that strange and different railway. At the start of the 1950s Weymouth station was quite impressive. It boasted a modest, overall roof, several platforms and quite a lot of activity, particularly on summer Saturdays.

A little way out from the station, alongside the main line, was a path which gave good viewing of events. Farther on was the depot, to which were allocated many GWR types, all in small numbers.

The spotter would see many 4-6-0s, mainly 'Halls', but the occasional 'Castle' or 'Grange' kept up the excitement. A pannier tank shunted the station and yards, while modest

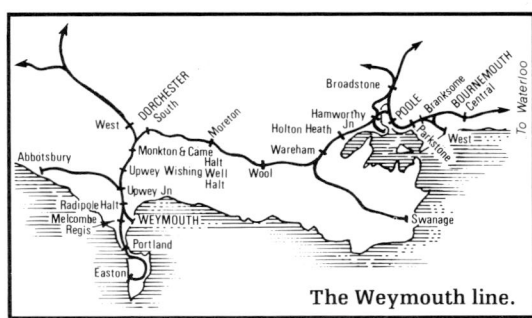

The Weymouth line.

Below:
In south Dorset chalk countryside BR Class 5 4-6-0 No 73037 plods sedately up Bincombe bank with the 14.11 from Weymouth to Waterloo on 27 February 1966. *Brian Stephenson*

Around Weymouth

Left:
Under the old Weymouth station roof in 1949, 'Castle' class 4-6-0 No 5066, then named *Wardour Castle*, rests after arrival from Paddington. The overall roof was removed in the early 1950s.

Below:
'Hall' class 4-6-0 No 6914 *Langton Hall* takes the 4.13pm to Paddington out of Weymouth station on 8 July 1956. *Mark Abbott*

Right:
Threading the streets on to Weymouth Quay on 31 May 1950 with a freight train is one of the bell-fitted Class 1366 0-6-0PTs. *J. C. Flemons*

Southern engines came and went. New 'West Countries' represented the SR with pride, and the occasional 'Merchant Navy' appearance vied with the 'Castles' for top place.

'O2' class 0-4-4Ts worked the branch to Portland and Easton, precariously engineered around the cliffs of Portland Bill.

To my young, Southern eyes, however, the oddest things were the stopping trains to Dorchester West and Maiden Newton. I remember '14xx' class 0-4-2Ts on push-pull trains vaguely, but strong in memory still are the diesel railcars. With some excitement I was invited into the cab of one — was it No W18? The line out of Weymouth climbed, first to call at Radipole Halt, then through the chalk hills to Upwey Junction where one occasionally saw an 0-4-2T and auto-train for the Abbotsbury branch. Climbing continued past Upwey Wishing Well Halt to Bincombe Tunnel and then it was downhill to Dorchester, where the Southern line swung off to the right.

It was a short walk from Dorchester West to the South station and its steam depot. SR locomotives working in the Weymouth area were based on Dorchester shed (to keep them off the Great Western!), a neat little depot that looked after its allocation well. The 'O2' 0-4-4Ts were polished though elderly, but the pride of place was held by the depot's three 'T9' 4-4-0s. I remember Nos 30117 and 30120 resplendent in shining BR lined black livery. The firm favourite was No 30119 which still carried malachite green, fully lined out in yellow and black with its number and 'British Railways' in shaded 'sunshine' lettering. The 'T9s' worked stopping trains between Weymouth and Bournemouth.

I remember well a trip behind No 30117. It arrived at Dorchester from Weymouth and, like all up trains, had to set its train back into the up platform which was, for historical reasons, on a different alignment from the main line. The three, red, ex-L&SWR non-corridor coaches looked ancient but clean behind the graceful 'Greyhound'.

First there was a short sprint to Moreton, and then came a magnificent gallop to Wool, and then to Wareham with a maximum of 64mph. Near Holton Heath station was a factory that frequently displayed two neat industrial saddle tanks. Beyond that, at Hamworthy Junction one could see the original Southampton and Dorchester main line which came in from Broadstone on the left, crossed, and curved southeast to reach Hamworthy, opposite Poole Quay. The 'T9' and its light load skirted round Poole harbour to reach Poole, and then began yet more hard work!

Out of Poole the line crosses Poole Park boating lake on a causeway and rises on an embankment over the town at a ruling grade of 1 in 60. The 1 in 50 start out of Parkstone station, halfway up the bank, was quite a test for a 'T9', but No 30117 chuffed manfully on up through the deep cutting reaching the summit gratefully at Branksome. I forget

Above:
Car traffic is a major problem on the Weymouth Quay branch in modern times. This 1983 view shows No 33.119 on a Waterloo-Weymouth Quay boat train held up while a policeman removes a Vauxhall Viva from its path.

whether we then finished at Bournemouth West or Central though the latter is, I think, more likely.

In time, as BR pursued its rationalisations, the Dorchester-Weymouth line became part of the Southern Region which then closed Dorchester shed and took over Weymouth depot. By then GW steam was disappearing in the face of diesel-hydraulics and DMUs. The '02s' had gone from the Portland line where now only the stone trains ran, hauled by '57xx' 0-6-0 pannier tanks. These saw the line through to its closure. The Western Region pulled back from competing with the Southern for London traffic. The line to Castle Cary became a singled shadow of its former self, carrying occasional Weymouth-Bristol services. Most of the halts closed and the Abbotsbury branch was but a memory. The branch to Weymouth Quay, once the haunt of small Class 1366 0-6-0PTs, was dieselised with Drewry 204hp mechanical shunters which pulled the boat trains through the

streets until much later the route was cleared for Class 33/1s to work right through.

In the last years of SR steam, Weymouth had its fair share with Bulleid Pacifics of all types predominant, and BR standard types in strength also. Indeed, on the last day of steam in July 1967, an unrebuilt 'West Country' worked through from Weymouth to Waterloo on an up express.

Lest one should imagine from all this that the Weymouth line is in decline, let me assure readers that today it is thriving beyond the imagination of all of us from the days of steam. Marketed under the 'Dorsetway' brand label, the hourly Bournemouth-Weymouth portions are well loaded, and the frequent eight-coach loads place great demands on the 1,550hp and four traction motors of Class 33/1s, particularly when propelling up the grades to Bincombe Tunnel. Indeed, eight coaches is more than many platform lengths can readily handle.

The discovery of oil in the 1960s at Wytch Farm near Furzebrook has brought new life on the freight side, too. Oil trains run daily to refineries around the UK. Even Hamworthy Quay is buoyant, with air-braked freight consignments adding to the air of comparative prosperity.

That is how is should be.

On Portland Bill

Dorset Royal

Above:
In its last years the Portland and Easton branch was worked by 0-6-0 pannier tanks which were ideal for the stone trains on this steeply graded line. No 7782 stands ready to depart from Easton with Portland stone blocks loaded in eight hyfits on 15 December 1956.

Below:
Pride of place in Dorchester's 1952 shed allocation was the ex-Royal 'T9' 4-4-0 No 30119, seen here still in malachite green livery on 29 June 1952.

Dorset Oil

From Poole to Bournemouth

Above:

Oil tanks have always been familiar at Wareham. It has a local distribution siding, and in modern times sees crude oil trains from the Wytch Farm field. In earlier days, 'M7' 0-4-4T No 30108 shunts a train on the up line. *Alan Wild*

Below:

The Weymouth line approaches Bournemouth on a causeway across Poole Park lake. 'Schools' 4-4-0 No 30912 *Downside*, having joined that route at Holes Bay Junction, brings a stopping train from the Old Road on to the foot of Parkstone bank on 3 April 1960.

Top:
The 1 in 50 of the upper part of Parkstone bank was normally taken in their stride by single engines on whatever load they were given. However, on 16 September 1956 an Ian Allan special from Weymouth was double-headed by 'T9' No 30727 piloting 'West Country' No 34106 *Lydford*

Above:
Branksome station was where the line from Weymouth split for Bournemouth West (left tracks in this picture) and Central. No 34106 *Lydford* pauses with the 10.00am from Weymouth to Waterloo on 14 April 1957.

Left:
No 76068 hurries a Weymouth to Waterloo train through pine tree topped cuttings towards Bournemouth Central.

Below:
Express trains from Bournemouth to Weymouth had to carry a headcode disc over each buffer because they traversed the Western Region after Dorchester. Diesel No 10000 has charge of the down 'Royal Wessex' portions to Swanage and Weymouth on 2 July 1954.

Changing station

Right:
The former station at Poole was photographed in March 1960 and was soon to be replaced by a modern structure slightly farther west.
Roy Panting

Below right:
The new Poole station down platform is crowded as No 33.117 arrives with the 13.35 from Waterloo to Weymouth in April 1983.

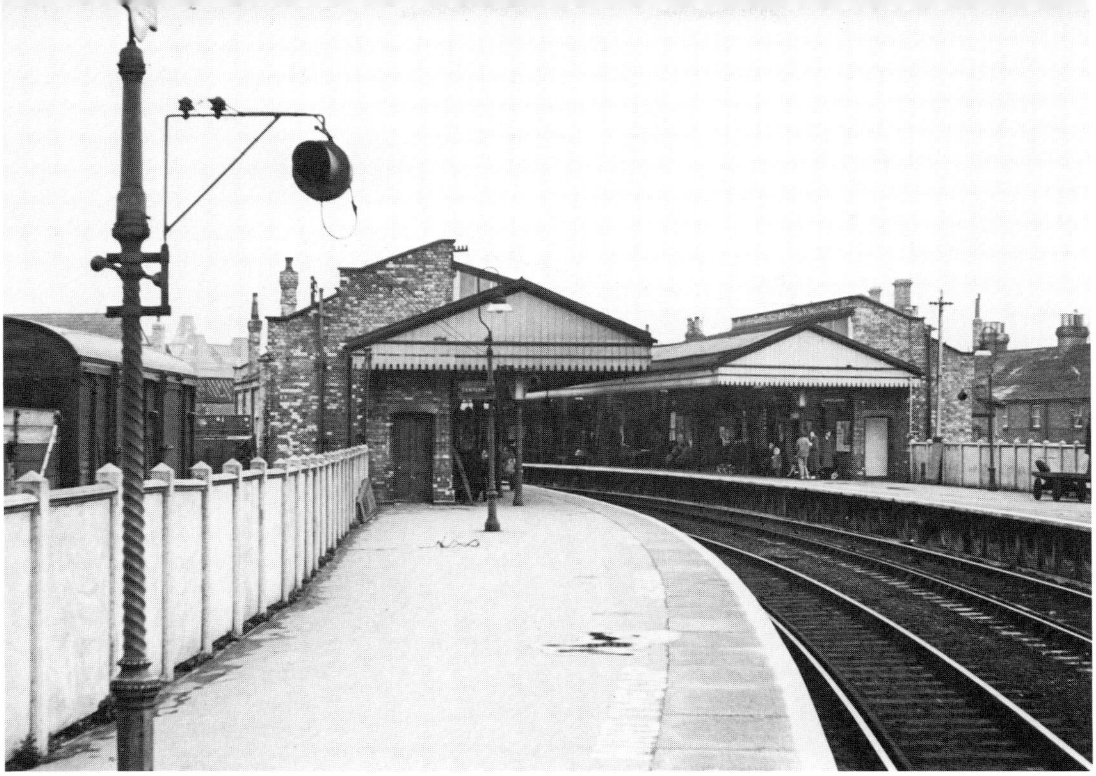

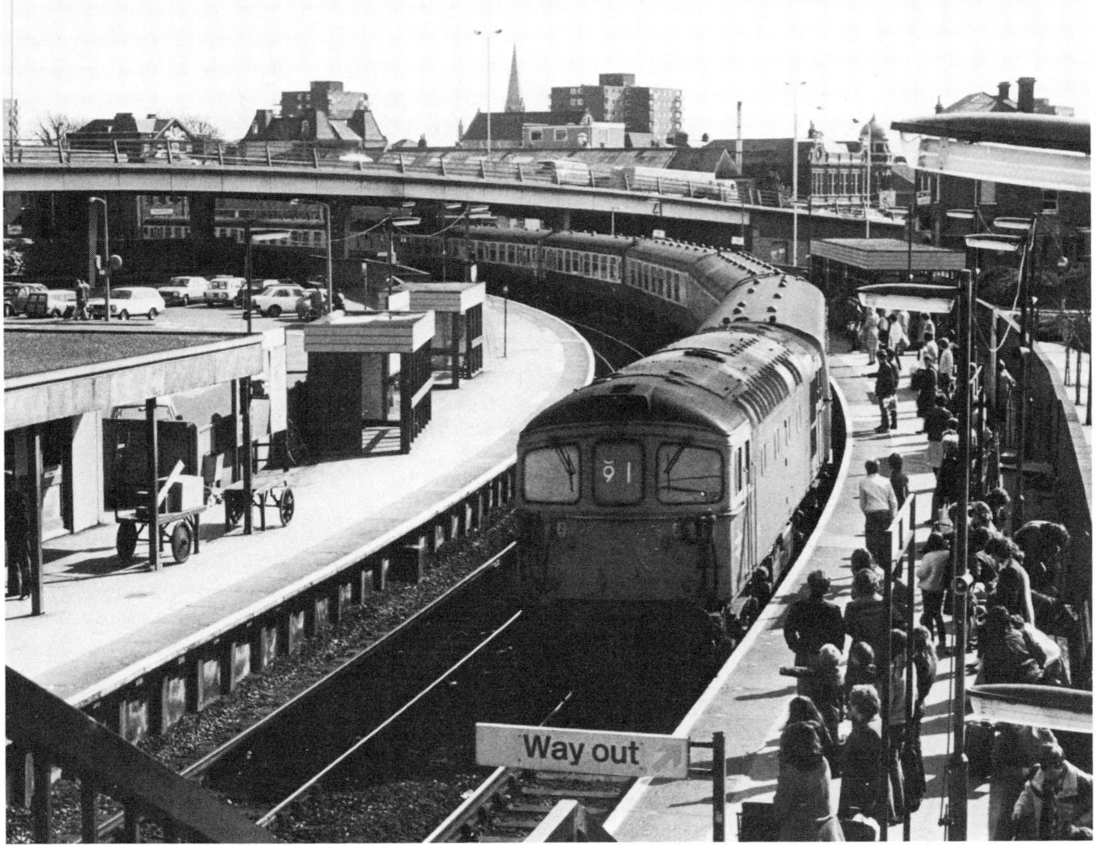
Way out

Over the Mendips

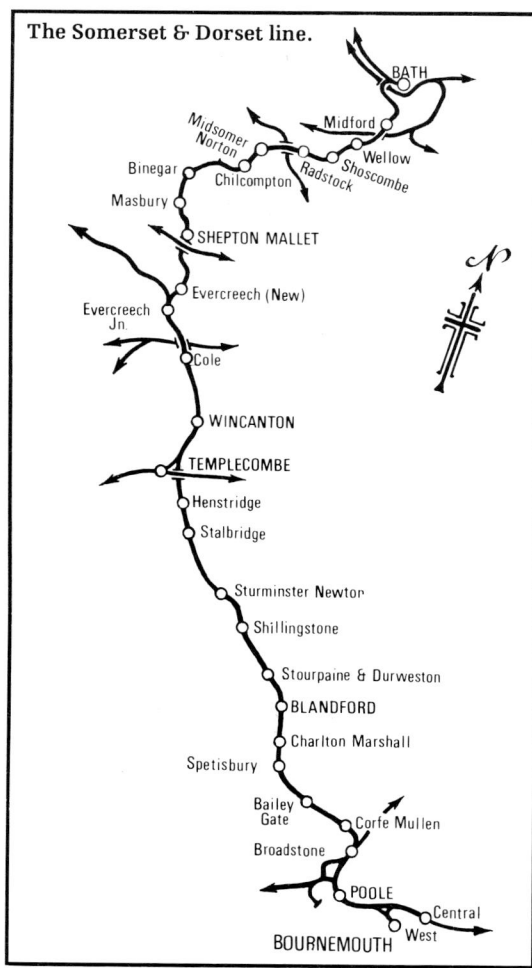

The Somerset & Dorset line.

It was a rather odd working arrangement that resulted in the LMS Class 5 4-6-0s being seen in such far apart places as Wick and Bournemouth. Bournemouth was not strictly on the LMS system at all.

After the 1923 grouping the Somerset & Dorset Joint Railway retained its semi-independent existence, but in 1930 it was formally absorbed as the joint responsibility of the Southern and LMS railways. The LMS provided all the locomotives and the Southern looked after the track, stations and local coaching stock. Coaches for through trains came from the LMS.

Under BR the line went to the Southern Region which took over Bath and Templecombe sheds. The SR obtained BR standard classes and deployed some 'West Countries' there, but also kept LMS types in service. Later the Western Region took charge north of Templecombe, and GW 0-6-0s and pannier tanks, together with WR ex-LMS '8F' 2-8-0s, were added to the variety.

The star turn on the line was definitely the 'Pines Express'. It was with some excitement that I took my Eastleigh friend one morning to join the 'Pines' at Bournemouth West. We had an unrebuilt 'West Country' with the usual 10 coaches, which ran briskly over the hump to Poole. West of Poole the train turned north off the Weymouth line, climbing to Broadstone where it manoeuvred across the original Southampton and Dorchester line to join the start of the S&D single line.

From Broadstone to Templecombe the line undulated, obviously constructed with a minimum of earthworks. At Evercreech Junction we paused, it seemed, to take breath and to prepare for the vicious climb ahead. An old LMS '2P' 4-4-0, its cylinder relief valves tinkling desultorily, backed on to the front of the Pacific as pilot.

The start from Evercreech is graphically and permanently etched on a superb record by Argo Transacord. A 'pip' from the '2P's' whistle is answered by a 'screech' from the Pacific. The two engines are gently opened up. The 'West Country' slips, its light, sharp exhaust in no way drowning the steady, deep, stentorian beat as the 4-4-0 rolls almost majestically ahead. Then it's heads out of the windows for the enthusiasts as the train climbs the grade, in some places approaching 1 in 50, on double track, briefly accelerating through Shepton Mallet before settling down again to around 25mph through the beautiful Mendip Hills. This is wonderful country. Pale stone villages and farms nestle in lush green valleys flanked by rolling hills.

The summit at Masbury was almost 900ft above sea level. Once over the top our train swept around curves at 60mph, the '2P' galloping steadily ahead of the swaying Bulleid Pacific. The approach to Bath was steeply downhill on single track, brakes

Above:
Preparing for the climb over the Mendips, '2P' 4-4-0 No 40569 has just coupled to No 73047 at the head of the northbound 'Pines Express' at Evercreech Junction on 6 April 1957. Note the tablet catcher at the ready on the '2P's' tender.

Below:
The '9Fs' were the only engines that could take full 12-coach loads over the S&D unaided. No 92204 prepares to leave Bournemouth West with a test train on 29 March 1960. *Alan Trickett*

Above:
BR Class 5 4-6-0 No 73050 rouses the echoes around Bournemouth West Junction on 19 May 1956 as it accelerates a relief to the northbound 'Pines Express' past Branksome depot.

Right:
The S&D line avoided Templecombe station and so a second engine was used to shuttle trains up and down the link to the station. 'Z' 0-8-0T No 30957 was photographed in 1957 with the 9.55am from Bath to Bournemouth. *Alan Trickett*

Below:
A quiet moment at Evercreech Junction in
September 1962 as a northbound freight leaves
behind '4F' 0-6-0 No 44560. *Alan Trickett*

grinding until, swinging to the right, we joined the LMS main line from Gloucester, passed the locomotive shed and gas works on the left, and rolled into the small terminus of Bath (Green Park). Our engines hooked off and a nondescript black '5' coupled to the other end of the train for the journey north to Manchester.

During most of the year the 'Pines Express' was the only heavy passenger train on the S&D. Other trains were often only three coaches, worked by anything from a '4F' 0-6-0 or '2P' 4-4-0 to BR Class 4 tender engines, a Pacific or Class 5.

On summer Saturdays however all peace was shattered. The popularity of Bournemouth as a holiday resort for northern Englanders necessitated a procession of heavy trains in both directions almost all day long. The morning departures from Bournemouth West were crossed on the S&D by southbound overnight trains. Trains came all day from Manchester, Liverpool, Bradford, Leeds, Derby and even Cleethorpes!

Everything that could move was called to help out. '9F' 2-10-0s were borrowed from the Western Region for the season. These excellent machines could take a full 12-coach train over the Mendips unaided. S&D Class 7F 2-8-0s were drafted on to passenger trains and these tough machines could handle 10 without help. The Class 5s and Bulleid Pacifics were only allowed eight coaches unaided and so required assistance on the holiday trains, pilots being normally drawn from the stud of '2Ps' and BR '4s'.

Summer Saturday

Below:
The holiday weekends brought countless extra Saturday trains to the Somerset & Dorset line. Nos 75072 and 34046 *Braunton* **double-head the 10.05am from Bournemouth West to Bradford past Windsor Hill on 4 August 1962.**

Bottom:
Class 5 No 44867 pilots rebuilt 'West Country' No 34029 *Lundy* **on the descent past Chilcompton with the Saturday 12.20pm Bournemouth West to Nottingham on 4 August 1962.**

Then came the age of the motor car and the summer specials were no longer required. The 'Pines Express' was diverted to a new route via Basingstoke and Reading to Birmingham and Manchester. The local traffic dwindled and closure came after many false attempts early in 1966. No longer did expresses fill in $2\frac{1}{4}$ hours over the 73 miles from Bournemouth to Bath.

The closure reduced grown men almost to tears. A local poet writing in Bournemouth Railway Club's magazine, BRC News, in March 1966 put our thoughts succinctly into verse:

Monday, 7-3-66
No more the lusty bark of 'Nines'
Forging northwards with the 'Pines',
Nor shout and roar of the faithful 'Two'
On nine full coaches bound for Crewe.
The points are clipped, the signals on,
And every single train has gone.

The bell of Beeching sounds its doom
And life departs from Templecombe.
At Evercreech, once busy Junction,
Everything has ceased to function.
The tunnels stand all draped in black,
Roofs dripping, like tears, on desolate track.

Rust descends on chairs and rails,
Broken windows tell their tales,
Dust lies thick on station floors
And only gusts of wind move doors.
The end has come: I stand aghast;
The Western Region's won at last.

Alan Thorpe

The Evening of the Star

Above:
An historic occasion was the day (8 September 1962) when the 'Pines Express' last traversed the Somerset & Dorset. On the very last train, the last-built BR steam locomotive No 92220 *Evening Star* (specially requested by the Bournemouth Railway Club) winds its way through the curves at Midford.

Bath Green Park

Above right:
'2P' 4-4-0 pilots '4F' No 44422 on the 7am from Cleethorpes to Exmouth out of Bath on 19 August 1961. This train used the S&D as far as Templecome. *Alan Trickett*

Right:
Stripped of much of its glazing, the overall roof of Bath Green Park station was nonetheless impressive. No 41241 is at the head of SR stock on a stopping train to Bristol on 6 April 1957.

Branch to Highbridge

Above:
The S&D had a long branch that meandered across the Somerset plain to Highbridge and Burnham-on-Sea. At Highbridge the branch train to Evercreech Junction waits in the bay with Class 3F 0-6-0 No 43218.

Below:
On 6 April 1957 the contents of the small locomotive shed at Highbridge were '3F' No 43216, an Ivatt 2-6-2T and a Midland '1P' 0-4-4T.

Branches

One day, in those childhood days when the sun always shone (or so one's memory inclines), a friend and I were playing near a railway line at Ashley Heath, just west of Ringwood. In the distance we could see a little green train coming towards us, strangely with the engine at the back. Not long after, another two-coach train, this time in red, came by, also with an 'M7' 0-4-4T as power.

This was what the Old Road, the original London to Dorchester main line, had been reduced to; in effect a double track country by-way served by infrequent push-pull trains plying between Brockenhurst, Ringwood, Wimborne, Broadstone and Bournemouth West. Even less frequent were the local freights which brought 0-6-0s of the L&SW Class 700, or sometimes Southern 'Qs', 'Q1s', or Moguls.

Left:
Alresford on the Winchester to Alton branch. 'M7' No 30029 arrives with a push-pull for Southampton Terminus on 2 November 1957, the last Saturday of full steam working on the branch, and passes an Ivatt 2-6-2T on an up train.

Locations of branch lines.

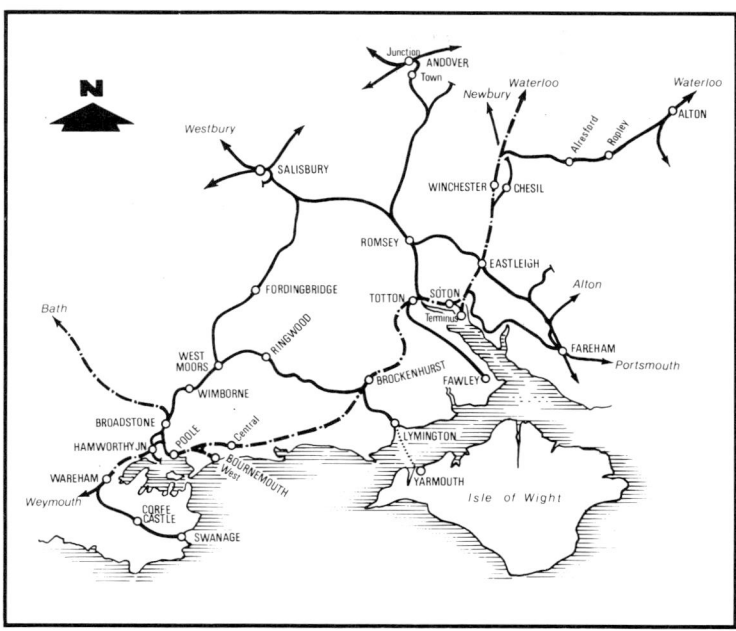

Old Road variety

Right:
On the last day of services on the Old Road, 2 May 1964, 'M7' 0-4-4T No 30480 leaves Ringwood with a train from Brockenhurst to Bournemouth.
Alan Trickett

Below:
'T9' 4-4-0 No 30287 took over the RCTS 'Wessex Wyvern' railtour at Brockenhurst and is seen here heading down the Old Road near Holmesley on 8 July 1956.

Bottom:
The Old Road was used on occasions for diverting main line trains. No 73082 *Camelot* passes Wimborne on the 9.35am from Waterloo to Bournemouth on 3 April 1960.

The Old Road did see occasional main line trains when the direct line was blocked and in summer the Channel Islands boat trains and other holiday specials were routed that way to avoid Bournemouth on their way to Weymouth.

Nonetheless the Old Road could boast a branch line. At West Moors a single track curved north to meander up the valley of the River Avon, through Fordingbridge and several villages, joining the Southampton-Salisbury line a few miles out of that cathedral city. When I first knew it, the Bournemouth-Salisbury stopping trains were a last stamping ground of the old Drummond 4-4-0s of Classes K10 and L11. I also saw 'S11s', 'L12s', 'T9s'. Unusually, just before the line closed, a batch of Maunsell/Wainwright Class E1 4-4-0s was drafted to Salisbury to work the route.

Other resorts in the area justified branch lines, of completely different characters. A bay platform at Wareham was the starting point of the Swanage branch trains. These were the familiar 'M7'-hauled push-pull trains, and would connect out of London-Weymouth trains which they would follow for a mile or so out to Worgret Junction before turning south. The single line branch crossed the flat land near the upper reaches of Poole harbour, past an area of clay pits. If the traveller thought he saw steam some distance from the railway towards the west he might not have been mistaken.

Then the train would plunge into the Purbeck Hills, past the mound surmounted by Corfe Castle before halting briefly at the station in the delightful grey stone village of the same name. Then on the engine would chuff, through green undulating land, to reach the small but pleasant seaside resort of Swanage. This even had a tiny locomotive shed among its classic Purbeck stone railway buildings. The push-pulls were later displaced by BR 2-6-4Ts, and lastly by Hampshire DEMUs, again only to reign for a short time before the line was closed to passenger traffic.

The northernmost section of the Swanage branch now has a new role. From Furzebrook, formerly the starting point of trainloads of clay, there now are despatched daily behind Class 33s trains of crude oil for refining. The southernmost part of the line is now operated as a preserved railway with steam. Who knows, we may see the whole length in operation again in the future.

Nearer to Bournemouth was the Hamworthy branch, for most of its time a freight-only line providing access to the Quay at Hamworthy, directly opposite Poole Quay. The Hamworthy branch was shunted by the neat Adams 0-4-0Ts of Class B4, while larger engines appeared on through freights. The 'B4' dock tanks were more at home on the Poole Quay branch. This ran through the streets from Poole station and enabled ships at the quayside to unload to rail.

While Poole Quay is now railless, Hamworthy is trading very well. A variety of freight uses the branch including motor car imports. Even Freightliner working has been tried here.

Of all the area's branches, only one still carries passengers today and to its credit it is electrified. Passengers to the Isle of Wight can board a Class 416 (2HAP) unit at Brockenhurst and are treated to a New Forest heath panorama before being taken gently around the harbour edge between Lymington Town and Harbour stations. Small Sealink ferries connect here with Yarmouth on the Island.

The Lymington branch was another line to be host to 'M7s' with two or three-coach push-pull trains. When the 'M7s' were worn out, Ivatt 2-6-2Ts did the job, though without the benefit of push-pull working.

This was another line which blossomed into major activity on summer Saturdays. Boat trains took holidaymakers from Waterloo to Lymington in their hundreds, to join the ferries to Yarmouth. The railway workings were interesting. As I first remember them light Pacifics worked them from London as far as Brockenhurst, and there they would give way to a 'Q' or 'Q1' 0-6-0 for the branch section. As the Pacifics were too long to turn on the Brockenhurst turntable they had to go to Bournemouth for this, not a very satisfactory arrangement. However, the turntable was big enough for a 'Schools' 4-4-0. When the 'Schools' were displaced by the Kent Coast electrification many went to Nine Elms for Western Section work, some thus returning to their prewar territory. The Lymington boat trains were entrusted to 'Schools' from the early 1960s, though as car ownership spread and BR consciously eased out of much seasonal traffic the Lymington boat trains soon outlived their demand and were withdrawn. Today the EMU connection, made up to four cars in summer, is more than adequate for the service.

Nearer to Southampton the single line Fawley branch is now a heavy oil artery, the Esso refinery there spawning up to 20 oil trains a day. Passenger trains no longer run, though formerly one could enjoy 'M7' 0-4-4Ts

By-way in Purbeck

Above:
Corfe Castle and Swanage stations were built in local Purbeck stone. This view of Corfe Castle station, taken in August 1966, shows the real castle almost hidden behind the trees on the right.
Roy Panting

Below:
An afternoon Wareham-Swanage train nears Corfe Castle behind 2-6-2T No 41312 on 25 August 1966. *L. A. Nixon*

hauling up to six non-corridor ex-L&SWR coaches before the DEMUs had their brief stay. Local freights used to be hauled by BR Class 3 2-6-2Ts, and there was a brief period when 'H16' 4-6-2Ts, and then Class W 2-6-4Ts held sway, having been displaced from cross-London freights by dieselisation. When the oil trains began in earnest, '9F' 2-10-0s from the London Midland Region worked them, to a distribution point at Bromford Bridge near Birmingham. Later Class 33 diesels took over, and Class 47s are now the principal power.

Apart from the Portsmouth-Salisbury lines which were very much the territory of 'U' and 'N' 2-6-0s and 'T9' 4-4-0s as well as the standard BR Class 4, Southampton was the originating point of Alton trains, usually 'M7' push-pulls or Ivatt 2-6-2Ts on three coaches. The Alton line branched off from the main line north of Winchester and pursued a steeply undulating course through pleasant Hampshire countryside, past watercress beds and

countless farms. Occasionally it was used as a diversion route from the main line. On these days it was normal for southbound trains to be double-headed out of Alton, the 1 in 40 climb towards Medstead & Four Marks being the steepest in the area covered by this book. Now it is the scene of one of the more enterprising preserved steam railways, which has concentrated on restoring locomotives of the types normally seen in those parts, though only the section from Alresford to Medstead is as yet open.

Yet another 'M7'-worked push-pull line was the Andover branch that left the Salisbury line just north of Romsey. That was a pleasant by-way which followed closely the meanderings of the River Test and so gained very little speed. It was the scene of the final heydays of branch line steam in the area.

The circumstances of this were unusual. In 1958 when diesel-electric multiple-units were being delivered a regular interval local services timetable was set up. Before all DEMUs had been delivered, two routes were steam hauled to the hourly interval required. 'T9' 4-4-0s worked three-coach trains between Portsmouth and Andover for a season. When later some more DEMUs had arrived, 'M7' 0-4-4Ts covered the Eastleigh-Andover section with push-pull trains. Thus did steam services have a brief Indian summer — at the price of a rise in hot boxes on the 60-year old 'M7s'.

Branch connection

Below:
'T9' 4-4-0 No 30702 stands in the up bay at Salisbury with a stopping train to Bournemouth West via West Moors, while No 35006 *Peninsular & Oriental SN Co* **starts away with an Exeter to Waterloo express on 27 April 1957.**

Freight only

Lymington for the Isle of Wight

Above:
At Hamworthy station, long since closed to passengers, 'B4' 0-4-0T No 30093 prepares to take freight up the branch to Hamworthy Junction.

Below:
After arrival of the ferry *Farringford* from Yarmouth, Class Q 0-6-0 No 30530 is ready to start from Lymington Pier with a Saturday boat train to Waterloo on 12 July 1958.

Above:
'Q' No 30530 arrives with the 3.30pm boat train from Lymington at Brockenhurst where it will hand over to a 'West Country' for the run to Waterloo. No 35022 has stopped on the down line with a semi-fast to Bournemouth.

Oil artery

Left:
Empty oil tanks for Fawley trundle across Trotts Lane crossing near Marchwood behind 'H16' class 4-6-2T No 30516.   *J. C. Haydon*

Below:
A typical Fawley branch passenger train approaches Eastleigh. 'M7' No 30032 has six ex-L&SWR non-corridor coaches in May 1955.

Pompey stopper

Mid-Hants revival

Above:
A slow train to Portsmouth leaves St Denys behind 'T9' 4-4-0 No 30288 on 24 April 1956.

Below:
In contrast to the almost timeless scene on page 71 is this 1979 view of 'N' 2-6-0 No 31874 entering Alresford after preservation of part of the Alton branch by the Mid-Hants Railway.

Cross-Country

It was always the Western Region's fault. So we were led to believe when discussing the timekeeping of the through trains from the North of England to Bournemouth in the 1950s. Certainly the southbound Birkenhead and Newcastle trains were frequently handed over to the Southern at Basingstoke more than 20min late, and often over 40.

Both trains had quite complicated routeings, which was probably the real problem. The Newcastle came south via York (from where in some winters it started), Pontefract, Sheffield, Nottingham, Leicester, Banbury, Oxford, and Reading West curve to reach the Bournemouth line at Basingstoke. The closure of the Great Central route in the mid-1960s caused the train's re-routeing, and now it comes south from York via Sheffield, Derby, Birmingham New Street, Coventry, Banbury, Reading (reverse) and terminates at Poole.

Birkenhead may sound a strange place to start a train to Bournemouth, but one easily

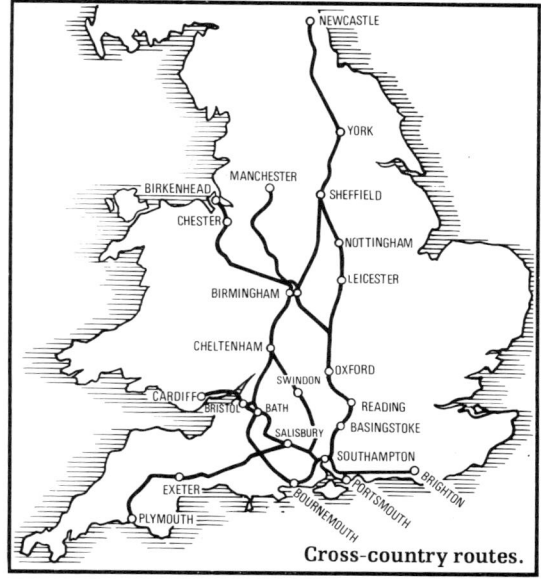

Cross-country routes.

Near journey's end, the through train from Newcastle to Bournemouth West approaches Gas Works Junction behind Western Region 4-6-0 No 6822 *Manton Grange* on 14 June 1958.

forgets that Liverpool was already well served with through trains or connections to the south coast. The Birkenhead came south through Chester, Shrewsbury, Birmingham Snow Hill, Banbury and Reading West. This train disappeared from the timetable around the period when the 'Pines Express' to Manchester was rerouted via Reading and Oxford in preparation for closing the Somerset & Dorset line.

Both trains changed engines at Oxford, Southern engines being used south thereof, except that the southbound Newcastle received an ex-GWR 'Hall' class 4-6-0. In the last months of steam after the GC line had closed this turn was in the hands of a LMR Class 5 4-6-0. The Birkenhead was generally the haunt of 'King Arthurs' including the wide-chimney Urie variety. Then, later, light Pacifics took over as the 'Arthurs' were scrapped.

After steam had gone there was a period when these inter-Regionals all but disappeared. However, the more vigorous management by BR of the northeast/southwest route and its many connecting links has had a spin-off in a recent escalation of through trains. The last four or five years has seen five or six such trains leaving Poole and Bournemouth daily. Class 47 haulage is now normal and timekeeping is good. Mk 1 coaching stock first gave way to early Mk 2, this in turn being replaced in 1982 by air-conditioned stock on most trains. Destinations include Newcastle, Liverpool, Manchester and Glasgow.

The cross-country train that brought to Southampton and Bournemouth the greatest variety of steam power over the years was not an inter-Regional train but was the daily through working from Brighton. In the early 1950s Marsh Atlantics were the staple power, interrupted on occasions by 'Schools' or three-cylinder 'U1' 2-6-0s. I remember seeing more than once Class B4X 4-4-0s; Nos 32060 and 32072 are numbers which spring to mind. For a time, some South Eastern 'L' class 4-4-0s appeared. When Brighton depot was particularly short, a BR or LM Class 4 2-6-4T was apt to appear, so this was always a train we enthusiasts would look out for. After the Atlantics' demise 'West Country' Pacifics reigned supreme.

The Brighton train's routeing was via Southampton to St Denys where it turned on to the Portsmouth line, calling at Fareham and Cosham before traversing the north side of the triangle there to take the coast line to Chichester, Barnham, Worthing and Brighton.

It was never a big train, usually between five and eight coaches. But it gave me two pleasant sights to remember for aye — a malachite green Atlantic glistening in the sun, and a 'Schools' resplendent in BR black with red, cream and grey lining. Somehow to me the big 4-4-0s looked their finest in shining black, though most would disagree I am sure, preferring the later BR green.

Nowadays the passenger from Bournemouth to Brighton faces two changes, at Southampton and Fratton. Maybe, one day, a third rail will be laid between St Denys and the Hilsea/Cosham triangle. Then a Class 423 EMU from Brighton would be a most welcome arrival at Bournemouth, would it not?

Another chapter has already made reference to the Portsmouth-Bristol trains via Southampton. Each day there used to be additionally a through train from Brighton to Plymouth. This was normally quite a heavy train for what is, after all, a somewhat hilly and curvaceous route, and was normally 'West Country' hauled. On occasions when Brighton depot's motive power problems were extreme, one might see a 'U1' 2-6-0 or even a BR 2-6-4T but these presumably did not work west of Salisbury.

In many ways the Bristol-Portsmouth route has seen more changes in the 20 years since dieselisation than before. Steam first gave way to Western Region diesel multiple-units of the mechanical variety, cross-country and InterCity types being used. Then, as the SR resisted DMUs, 'Hymek' diesel-hydraulics took over with locomotive hauled stock. Some services later saw SR DEMUs penetrate to Bristol. Then the WR responded with Class 31s on coaching stock, these in turn being usurped by SR Class 33s. At least the major problem with the steam workings has disappeared — locomotives no longer have to be changed at Salisbury!

One long-forgotten cross-country route, which I never experienced in its entirety, was that which took trains of SR locomotives and WR stock from Southampton to Cheltenham. Either a Maunsell or BR Class 4 2-6-0 would take three coaches to Andover Junction, then straddle the west of England main line to reach the former Midland & South Western Junction Railway which headed via Savernake to Swindon Town. Thence it crossed over the GWR main line and meandered northwest until it eventually reached Cheltenham. Later, through workings ceased and the line was reached by changing at Andover Junction into a WR set hauled by a Churchward 2-6-0 or 2-6-2T.

Variety on the Newcastle

Above:
For several years the normal power for the Newcastle-Bournemouth train southbound from Oxford was an ex-GW 'Hall' class locomotive. On 11 June 1958 No 6970 *Whaddon Hall* leaves Eastleigh.

Below:
Later, when the train was rerouted via Birmingham, LM Region Class 5s were common. No 45046 lifts the Newcastle to Poole train across the New Forest heath between Lymington Junction and Sway on 26 June 1965. In the background the Lymington branch train can be seen approaching the junction. *Alan Trickett*

'Pines' rerouted

Top:
A week after its removal from the Somerset & Dorset line, on 15 September 1962, the northbound 'Pines Express' enters Christchurch station behind 'Battle of Britain' No 34085 *501 Squadron*.

Diesels across country

Above:
The end of steam brought WR diesel-hydraulics to the main line cross-country trains, such as No D7068 seen here passing Eastleigh in 1969 with a Southampton to Birmingham train.

Left:
Later, Class 47s became the regular power on the inter-Regionals. No 47.432 climbs the 1 in 50 of Parkstone bank on 8 April 1983 with the 17.05 from Poole to Birmingham.

The Brighton link

The graceful lines of Brighton Atlantic No 32425 *Trevose Head* are picked out by sunshine as she blows off prior to departure from Bournemouth Central with the through train to Brighton in the mid-1950s. *Alan Trickett*

Above:
One of the rare engines brought to Bournemouth by the Brighton train was three-cylinder Class U1 2-6-0 No 31891, seen on 8 June 1951 resting at Bournemouth depot during the longer Sunday layover.

Below:
The Brighton to Plymouth through train leaves Southampton on 17 April 1956 behind No 34046 *Braunton*.

Via Salisbury

Odd routeing

Above:
One of the ex-River Class U 2-6-0s No 31791, leaves Southampton Central with ex-GW stock forming a Portsmouth to Cardiff train on 25 May 1957.

Above right:
After changing engines at Salisbury on 27 April 1957, ex-GW 4-6-0 No 5923 *Colston Hall* prepares to leave with a Cardiff train.

Below:
Despite the short distance from Branksome, Somerset & Dorset engines were rare indeed at Bournemouth Central. '4F' 0-6-0 No 44417 had arrived with a football special from Plymouth via Templecombe to Boscombe on 12 April 1958.

They also served

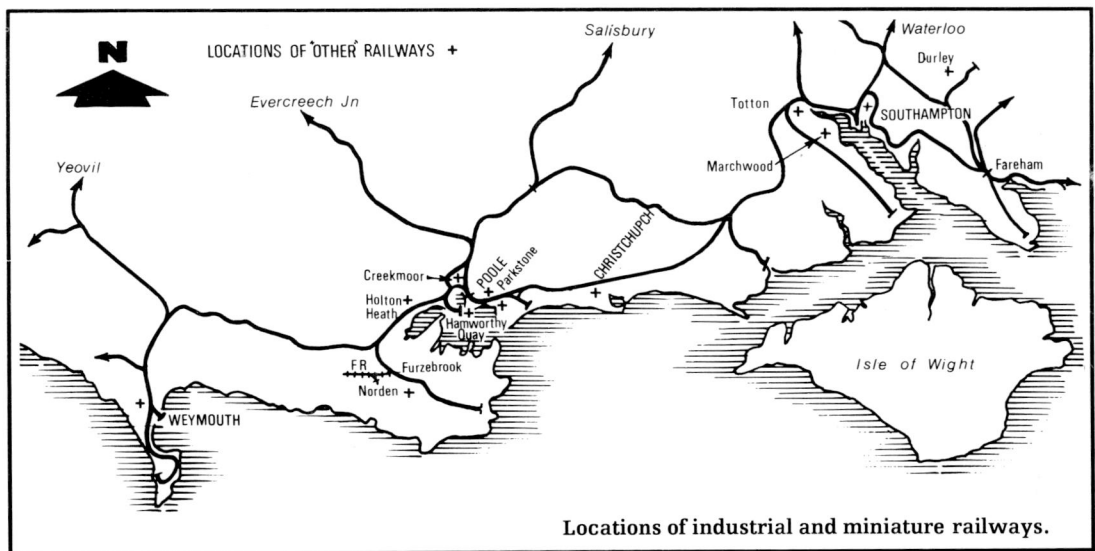

Locations of industrial and miniature railways.

One sunny afternoon a youth cycled to Parkstone station to watch the efforts of SR and LMS locomotives climbing the 1 in 60/50 of the bank from Poole causeway to the outskirts of Branksome. He watched a 'T9' chirpily bowl up the hill with five coaches, to be followed later by a '2P' on a three-coach stopper off the S&D. The '2P' seemed to make heavy weather of it, though perhaps our observer can be forgiven some bias.

During a lull in the traffic, the sound of a steam engine working hard but slowly could be heard. Nothing could be seen coming from either direction, which was odd. Imagine the youth's surprise when steam appeared between the trees behind the houses at the south side of the station, and a delightful 0-4-0 saddle tank chuntered through an open gate into the down goods yard with two open wagons. *George Jennings* was a 1902 Peckett, very clean, light green, with polished brass safety valve cover and nameplates.

Back on his cycle, our observer soon traced the single line for about $\frac{1}{4}$-mile to the George Jennings pottery. On the way he espied a narrow gauge track which climbed out of a quarry and crossed the standard gauge on the flat. A small Simplex 0-4-0 sputtered up from the quarry with a string of clay wagons for

the pottery. So there was the system — clay from the quarry, processed in the pottery, and the products loaded on to BR wagons and transferred on the private railway to Parkstone goods yard for collection by a BR pick-up freight.

Now the quarry and goods yard are covered by grass and modern housing, and the branch line is difficult to follow. In the 1950s it was all there, and by the 1970s, no trace.

Traces are growing over, too, of the very much more extensive system of clay railways in the area between Wareham and Corfe Castle in Dorset. Pike Brothers, Fayle & Co ran a 2ft 8in gauge network that linked clay mines in the Purbecks with the BR exchange sidings at Furzebrook and to wharves on the western edge of Poole harbour. When I first saw the railway in 1955 the wharf lines had gone, though a derelict engine shed survived. Furzebrook itself was a hive of activity, there being four working steam locomotives based there.

Tertius was a Manning Wardle 0-6-0ST that had acquired a boiler from a wider gauge engine of former years. Consequently the firebox sat across the frames, the boiler was pitched high, and the whole had a tall, almost

foreign appearance. *Tertius* that day was working the line westwards from Furzebrook to a focal point from where tracks appeared to trail off in all directions. A roar from the background indicated the approach of neat, green Peckett 0-4-2ST *Sextus*, climbing up with a load of newly mined clay.

Then began what looked to the uniniatited like a highly dangerous operation. *Sextus* backed its short train very hard down a siding and fly-shunted the end wagon which had a man riding on it holding the brake lever. As it approached the end of the track the brake was applied on the fleeing wagon and the wagon body tipped forward, dropping its load

of clay over the edge into the drying beds. The empty wagon was then placed on another line and the procedure was repeated with each of the other wagons of the train.

Another engine, clearly tired from having recently been through the same performance, was resting nearby. This was *Quintus*, a beautiful Manning Wardle 0-4-0ST. Only *Septimus* was not in steam that day, lying dormant in Furzebrook shed. Shortly before my visit, the line's oldest engine, the well-tank *Secundus*, had been moved to the Birmingham Museum of Science & Industry. Not many years after, all the system had closed.

Another engine that is now preserved elsewhere was for a time resident in Dorset. The Welsh Highland Railway 2-6-2T *Russell* spent some years on the Norden Quarry system near Corfe. It was minus its leading pony truck for curvature reasons, but was too heavy for the track and did little work there.

Opposite Poole quay where BR's 'B4' dock tank held reign, was Hamworthy quay where coastal steamers loaded and unloaded export and import goods. Two Robert Stephenson & Hawthorn 0-4-0STs shunted here, both light green and usually kept in shiny condition. *Bonnie Prince Charlie* and *Western Pride* carried 1948 building plates. The former, when steam was displaced from the wharf, ended up at the Didcot Railway Centre.

The fate of the two saddle tanks that could sometimes be glimpsed in the ordnance factory at Holton Heath, or of the 0-4-0ST near Creekmoor, I cannot relate.

Southampton had its share of steam worked industrial locations. Burtt, Boulton & Heywood's timber works at Totton used a bright green Barclay 0-4-0ST for many years. Three Peckett 0-4-0STs were to be found among the wharves behind the Northam to Terminus line. One, at Chapell Tramway, was later replaced by the small Barclay 0-4-0ST *Lord Fisher*, now preserved. The other two, at Corrall's wharf, were displaced by ex-BR Class B4 0-4-0T No 30096 then named *Corrall Queen*. This latter used to be glimpsed from BR at times as it emerged from behind Northam gasworks when transferring wagons to BR.

A little farther afield, off the Fawley branch, was the large Marchwood military establishment. Transport around this was to be had by rail, using a lovingly cared for standard austerity 0-6-0ST called *Waggoner* and ex-BR standard non-corridor coaches. In the author's recollection this engine was the last steam locomotive to see regular service on the railways in the Bournemouth and Southampton area. It left the area for Shoeburyness in 1982.

Although it started operations near the end of this album's period, the Hampshire Narrow Gauge Society only got its Bagnall 0-4-0ST *Wendy* working in 1980. The line is based at Four Winds, Durley, near Southampton.

A major mystery is the disappearance of the miniature railway steam locomotives of the area. The first time I went to Weymouth, there was a super little 'A2/2' Pacific there. In

Narrow gauge in the clay pits

Left:
During transfer work on the Furzebrook Railway in 1955, Manning Wardle 0-6-0ST *Tertius* poses across a road near Furzebrook village.

Below:
Peckett 0-4-2ST *Sextus* brings up newly mined clay for dumping on the drying beds which can be seen in the left mid-background. The Furzebrook Railway ran on 2ft 8in gauge.

Right:
Pausing between duties, *Quintus* of the Furzebrook Railway stands in the Dorset summer sunshine in 1955.

Below:
More typical of the traction on the Dorset clay lines was this four-wheeled internal combustion locomotive seen in 1955 at Furzebrook.

Bottom:
The ex-Welsh Highland Railway 2-6-2T *Russell* stands unwanted at Norden in 1955.

1970 the resident engine was *John of Gaunt*, a high-boilered Atlantic which I have since seen on the Stapleford Park Railway in the East Midlands. Christchurch had a small line which ran round a car park near the harbour, with a $10\frac{1}{4}$in gauge model of streamlined 'Coronation' No 6220.

The best local miniature railway was (and is) undoubtedly that which runs round the lake in Poole park. In delightful surroundings, from 1946 one could watch 4-4-2 No 1001 *Vanguard* clank its leisurely way on quite a lengthy circuit. Two diesels of strangely Western Region outline had taken over 25 years later.

Although most of these little engines are now but a memory, all these smaller steam locomotives provided us with an alternative source of considerable interest. They deserve their place in this book, even though at its end!

Poole industrials

Above:
Hamworthy quay was shunted by two 1949-built Robert Stephenson & Hawthorn 0-4-0STs. This one was *Bonnie Prince Charlie*, **photographed in 1958.**

Below:
A Bagnall 0-4-0ST (2596 of 1938) at Holton Heath on 17 July 1959.   *Roy Panting*

Steam around Southampton

Above:
This Barclay 0-4-0ST was run by Burtt, Boulton & Heywood to service their timber treatment works near Totton. 1958.

Below left:
Chappell Tramways' Peckett 0-4-0ST is seen in its shed near Southampton Terminus, in 1959.

Top right:
The replacement for the two Pecketts at Corrall's Wharf was ex-BR 'B4' 0-4-0T No 30096, which they named *Corrall Queen*. It is seen here on 2 April 1966. *John H. Bird*

Centre right:
Army austerity 0-6-0ST No 92 *Waggonner* was photographed at Marchwood in 1976 when it was the last non-preserved active steam locomotive in the area. *Alan Thorpe*

Narrow gauge at Durley

Right:
The Hampshire Narrow Gauge Society's Bagnall 0-4-0ST *Wendy* was photographed recently running on the Durley Light Railway. *Allan Baker*

Steam in Miniature

Left:
This 10¼in gauge 'A2/2' Pacific ran on the Weymouth Miniature Railway in the early 1950s.
Ian Allan Library

Below:
The original locomotive on the Poole Park Miniature Railway was 4-4-2 *Vanguard*, seen here on 18 June 1955 when the line had been running nine years.

Bottom:
No 6220 *Coronation* was represented by this blue 10¼in Pacific which used to circumnavigate a car park near Christchurch harbour. *Roy Panting*

Appendices

Sunday afternoon at Bournemouth shed on
28 February 1954, showing the following classes:
'West Country', 'N15', 'M7', 'Q', 'B4' and 'T9'.

Steam locomotive depot allocations in 1950

Bournemouth

M7	30028/40/51/52/57/59/104/106/111/ 112/131/251/318/379
B4	30086/87/93
02	30204/212
G6	30260
S11	30398/403/404
Q	30548/549
700	30695
T9	30728
N15	30736/737/740/741/743/746/750/ 751/754
LN	30861-865
U	31622/32, 31795
WC	34093-95, 34105-109

Total 52

Dorchester

T9	30116/284/307/338
G6	30162
02	30177/179/197/223/229/231
S11	30399
L12	30415/424

Total 14

Eastleigh

M7	30029, 30031-33, 30048/53/109/ 125/128/242/357/378/479/673/ 674
B4	30082/83/89
T9	30121/282/286/287/300/304/313/ 705/708/711/713/721/722/729
L11	30148, 30154-157, 30159/171/173/ 175/411/413/437/442
02	30213/225/233
700	30306/316/350/700
T1	30367
S11	30401

L12	30422/423, 30429-434
D15	30463-472
H15	30473-475, 30477/478/483/489/ 491, 30521-524
Q	30530-532, 30535/536/542/543/ 544
0395	30566/571
C14	30588/589
N15	30749/752/772/777/779/783/784/ 785/788/789/790
LN	30850-857
Z	30950/952/956
P	31325
N	31828/66/67
E1	32133/47
E4	32491/92, 32510, 32557-59, 32562/ 63/79
Q1	33017-25

Total 142

Southampton Docks

USA	30061-74
E1	32156, 32606

Total 16

Weymouth

1366	1367/68/70
14xx	1453/54/67
1501	1789
4073	4080
45xx	4507/20/27/62
49xx	4930/88, 5978, 6902/12/45
43xx	5328/38/59/84
6959	6988/93
74xx	7408
57xx	9642

Total 26

Steam locomotive depot allocations at the end of steam on 9 July 1967

Bournemouth

WC	34004/24/25
LM2	41224/320
BR4	76005-7, 76009/11/26/67
BR4T	80011/134/146

Total 15

Eastleigh

USA	30064/67/69/71
WC	34037/60/87/90/93/95/102
BR4	75074-77
BR4	76064/66
BR4T	80016/139/152

Total 20

Weymouth
(No allocation by the time closed on 9 July 1967)

Below:
Final line-up on the last day. Fifteen steam locomotives whose services were no longer required were photographed at Weymouth depot on 9 July 1967. *Alan Thorpe*